English Grammar in Use Supplementary Exercises

with answers

Louise Hashemi
with Raymond Murphy

CAMBRIDGE
UNIVERSITY PRESS

CAMBRIDGE UNIVERSITY PRESS
Cambridge, New York, Melbourne, Madrid, Cape Town, Singapore,
São Paulo, Delhi, Dubai, Tokyo

Cambridge University Press
The Edinburgh Building, Cambridge CB2 8RU, UK

www.cambridge.org
Information on this title: www.cambridge.org/9780521755481

First published 2004
6th printing 2009

Printed in Italy by L.E.G.O. S.p.A.

A catalogue record for this publication is available from the British Library

ISBN 978-0-521-75548-1 English Grammar in Use Supplementary Exercises with answers
ISBN 978-0-521-75549-8 English Grammar in Use Supplementary Exercises without answers
ISBN 978-0-521-53289-1 English Grammar in Use with answers
ISBN 978-0-521-53290-7 English Grammar in Use without answers
ISBN 978-0-521-53762-9 English Grammar in Use with answers and CD-ROM
ISBN 978-0-521-53760-5 English Grammar in Use CD-ROM for Windows (single user)
ISBN 978-0-521-53761-2 English Grammar in Use Network CD-ROM (30 users)

Contents

To the student

English Grammar in Use Supplementary Exercises is for intermediate and advanced students who want extra practice in grammar, without help from a teacher.

There are 200 exercises in this new edition. Each exercise relates to a unit or units in *English Grammar in Use new edition 2004*, with the unit number(s) at the top of the page. All the answers are given in the Key (pages 121–136). Some exercises ask you to use your own ideas. For these, you can check the *Example answers* in the Key. You can use this book if you don't have *English Grammar in Use*, but for an explanation of the grammar points, you need to check in *English Grammar in Use*.

The grammar points covered in the book are *not* in order of difficulty, so you can go straight to the parts where you need the most practice. Where there are several exercises on one grammar point, however, the easier ones come first. It's a good idea to do each exercise, check your answers and then go on to the next one.

Many of the exercises are in the form of emails, letters, conversations or short articles. You can use these as models for writing or speaking practice.

To the teacher

English Grammar in Use Supplementary Exercises offers extra practice of most of the grammar points covered in *English Grammar in Use new edition 2004*. Much of the language is contextualised within dialogues, emails, letters, articles etc., encouraging students to consider meaning as well as form. The book can be used as self-study material or as a basis for further practice in class or as homework.

The book is designed for students who have already worked through the exercises in *English Grammar in Use* (or elsewhere) which are relevant to their needs, but who need more, or more challenging, practice. It is particularly useful for revision work.

The exercises are organised in the same order as the units of *English Grammar in Use*, and the numbers of the relevant *English Grammar in Use* units are shown at the top of each page. Within each group of exercises there is a progression from easier to more challenging, including exercises where students are encouraged to use their own ideas. The contextualised exercises can be used as models or springboards for speaking and writing practice of a freer nature.

Thanks

The authors would like to thank Alison Sharpe of Cambridge University Press for advice and support during the writing of this new edition, and Liz Driscoll for great editing and many helpful suggestions. Also, everyone at Kamae for their creative design work.

For trying out exercises and offering valuable comments on the original edition, thanks go to: students and staff at The British Council Young Learners' Centre, Barcelona, Spain, Anglo World, Cambridge, The Studio School, Cambridge, The International Language Academy, Cambridge, Lelio Pallini, Jon Butt, Cemille Iskenderoglu, Isidro Almándarez, Catherine Carpenter, Marco Palladino.

For providing feedback for the new edition, thanks go to: Margarida C.T. Busatto, Katie Head, Aleya Mokhtar, Graham Palmer, Rob Waring.

Photographic Acknowledgements
(top = *t*, bottom = *b*, left = *l*, right = *r*)

(credits still to come for 3 unconfirmed pictures 34tr, 95, 99b)

Alamy pp 30, 87, 51, 95; Anthony Blake Photo Library p 70*b* (Graham Kirk); www.JohnBirdsall.co.uk p 15; The Bridgeman Art Library p 63 (Pablo Picasso (1881–1973), *Guernica*, 1937 (oil on canvas. Museo Nacional Centro de Arte Reina Sofia, Madrid, Spain © Succession Picasso/DACS 2003; Collections pp 73 (Simon Warner), 99*t* (Mike Kipling); Corbis pp 10 (Tom & Dee Ann McCarthy), 20 (Adam Woolfitt), 24*b* (John Henley), 34*bl* (Joseph Sohm), 34*br* Dave G. Houser), 34*tl* (Rachel Royse), 63 (3/Dallas and John Heaton), 63 (6/film *Tomb Raider* by Simon West, Angelina Jolie in the role of Lara Croft. © Corbis/Sygma), 63 (7/Charles E. Rotkin), 116*t* (Kevin Fleming), 117*b* (Ashley Cooper), 117*t* (Jose Luis Pelaez, Inc); Getty Images pp 9 (Hulton Archive), 14 (Harald Sund), 19 (Howard Kingsnorth), 21 (Allsport Concepts/Pascal Rondeau), 52 (Paul Thomas), 65 (Simon Battensby), 70*t* (Mel Yates), 83 (Steve Satushek), 96 (Kyoko Hamada), 109 (Alan Thornton), 116*b* (Juan Silva); © David Hockney Studio/© Tate, London 2003 p 3; The Kobal Collection p 63 (film *The Seven Samurai* Director Akira Kurosawa, 1954); Rex Features p 24*t* (Paul Brown); By kind permission of Scholastic Children's Books, p 63 Philip Pullman, *Northern Lights*, © Philip Pullman 1995; Science Photo Library pp 4 (Fred Espenak), 6*b* (Bernhard Edmaier), 6*t* (Gregory Dimijian), 63 (1/Worldsat International), 63 (8/Philippe Plailly), 63 (10/Philippe Plailly/Eurelios); Topfoto pp 63 (Science Museum, London), 68 (Max Mumby ©2003 Topham/FNP)

Commissioned photography by MM Studios pp 63, 110

Picture research by Suzanne Williams

English Grammar in Use Supplementary Exercises

with answers

Present continuous and present simple
(I am doing and I do)

1 Complete the programme with the present continuous form of the verbs from the box.

| hold   offer   organise   ~~perform~~   play   sing |

What's on in Hampton this week?

Theatre Royal
The Hampton Drama society (1) _is performing_
As You Like It by William Shakespeare.
Wednesday – Saturday 7.30 pm.

The City Concert Hall
Simon Lee and Martha Glassen (2) ....
songs from operas by Mozart, Verdi and Puccini on Friday at 7 pm.

Hampton Sports Stadium
The college football team (3) ....
against a touring team from Germany at 2 pm on Saturday.

Market Square
Local farmers (4) .... their
monthly market this Sunday from 10 am to 2 pm.

Shopping Mall
All clothes shops (5) ....
discounts to shoppers before 11 am every day this week.

City Museum
The education department (6) ....
three special children's days – on Tuesday, Wednesday and
Thursday – for 8 to 12 year olds.
For more details, phone the City Information Office 292936

2 Complete the sentences with the present continuous form of the verbs.

A WENDY: Hi, Janice.
   JANICE: Hello, Wendy! (1) ..._Are you waiting_... (you / wait) for the London train?
   WENDY: No, I (2) .... (meet) my mother off the train from Bristol.

B MANDY: (3) .... (my radio / disturb) you?
   JAMES: No, not at all. I (4) .... (enjoy) the music.

C TOM: (5) .... (anyone / use) this room today?
   ELLEN: The marketing managers (6) .... (have) a meeting
here this afternoon, but it's free this morning.

D NINA: Why (7) .... (those people / shout)?
   GRAHAM: They (8) .... (demonstrate) against low wages.

E BEN: (9) .... (you / apply) for the manager's job when he
retires?
   COLIN: (10) I .... (consider) it, but I haven't decided yet.

F SALLY: (11) .... (Jane / leave) work early today?
   SUE: Yes, she (12) .... (fly) to Brussels at five o'clock.

G TIM: (13) .... (you / come) to the party on Thursday?
   BILL: No, I (14) .... (work) late, unfortunately.

3 Complete the description with the present continuous form of suitable verbs. Use the negative where necessary.

Mr and Mrs Clark and Percy by David Hockney, 1970

This is a painting of two people and their cat. Mr Clark (1) ....*is sitting*.... on a chair. Mrs Clark (2) .... near him. They (3) .... at each other, but at the viewer. Mrs Clark (4) .... a long dress. Mr Clark's got trousers and a jumper, but he (5) .... shoes. Percy is on Mr Clark's lap and he (6) .... something in the garden. The sun (7) .... outside, but the room is a bit dark. We can see part of a picture which (8) .... on the wall behind Mrs Clark. There's a vase of lilies on the table, and a book (9) .... beside it.

4 Choose a picture or photograph you like and describe what is happening in it.

....

....

....

....

....

....

....

....

5 Complete the text with the present simple form of the verbs.

What is an eclipse?

A solar eclipse (1) ..._happens_... (happen) when the moon
(2) .... (pass) in front of the sun. This only
(3) .... (take) place when there is a new moon.
It (4) .... (last) for up to 7.5 minutes.
　　During a solar eclipse, it is dark. The birds (5) ....
(not sing), and animals (6) .... (keep) still and quiet.
A solar eclipse (7) .... (not happen) very often, and most
people (8) .... (enjoy) seeing one. However, it's important not to look
straight at the sun. If you (9) .... (not remember) this, you can damage
your eyes.
　　A lunar eclipse (10) .... (occur) when the earth's shadow
(11) .... (fall) on the moon. The moon (12) .... (look)
dim until it (13) .... (come) out from the shadow.

6 Complete the questions with the present simple form of the verbs.

1　Which day of the week ..._do you go_... (you / go) to yoga class?

On Thursdays.

2　What time .... (the post / come)?

About 9.30.

3　.. (your sister / have) a mobile?

Yes, I can give you her number.

4　How often .... (you / see) your brother?

Nearly every weekend.

5　Why .... (you / travel) to work by bus?

Because it's cheaper than the train.

6　Where .... (your secretary / keep) the spare discs?

In that box beside the printer.

7　.. (you / want) a cold drink?

No thanks, I've just had one.

8　How many hours .... (you / work) in a week?

About thirty-five, usually.

9　How long .... (you / spend) on your homework?

At least one hour every evening.

10　.. (the paper shop / sell) stamps?

Yes, you can get some there.

7 Choose the correct alternative.

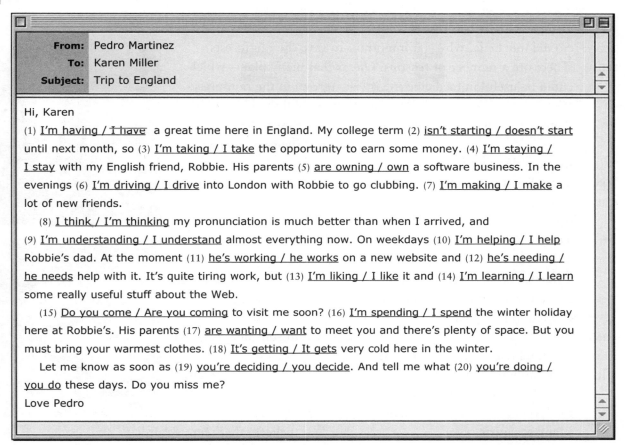

From: Pedro Martinez
To: Karen Miller
Subject: Trip to England

Hi, Karen

(1) <u>I'm having</u> / <s>I have</s> a great time here in England. My college term (2) <u>isn't starting / doesn't start</u> until next month, so (3) <u>I'm taking / I take</u> the opportunity to earn some money. (4) <u>I'm staying / I stay</u> with my English friend, Robbie. His parents (5) <u>are owning / own</u> a software business. In the evenings (6) <u>I'm driving / I drive</u> into London with Robbie to go clubbing. (7) <u>I'm making / I make</u> a lot of new friends.

(8) <u>I think / I'm thinking</u> my pronunciation is much better than when I arrived, and (9) <u>I'm understanding / I understand</u> almost everything now. On weekdays (10) <u>I'm helping / I help</u> Robbie's dad. At the moment (11) <u>he's working / he works</u> on a new website and (12) <u>he's needing / he needs</u> help with it. It's quite tiring work, but (13) <u>I'm liking / I like</u> it and (14) <u>I'm learning / I learn</u> some really useful stuff about the Web.

(15) <u>Do you come / Are you coming</u> to visit me soon? (16) <u>I'm spending / I spend</u> the winter holiday here at Robbie's. His parents (17) <u>are wanting / want</u> to meet you and there's plenty of space. But you must bring your warmest clothes. (18) <u>It's getting / It gets</u> very cold here in the winter.

Let me know as soon as (19) <u>you're deciding / you decide</u>. And tell me what (20) <u>you're doing / you do</u> these days. Do you miss me?

Love Pedro

8 Choose words from the box and make sentences ending as shown. Use verbs in the present continuous or present simple and any other words you need.

I	My best friend	My boss	My boyfriend	My classmates	My family
My father	My sister	My wife	None of my friends	Our children	
Our next-door neighbour	Our teacher	Several of my colleagues			

1 .....My boyfriend is studying for his final exams... this term.
2 .....My sister doesn't go to the cinema.. very often.
3 .....My classmates aren't talking much... right now.
4 ....this year.
5 .... every week.
6 .... at the moment.
7 .... this year.
8 .... at weekends.
9 .... this term.
10 .... right now.

9   Put the verbs into the correct form: present continuous or present simple.

Tony Hunt, a journalist, is interviewing Leila Markham, an environmental scientist.

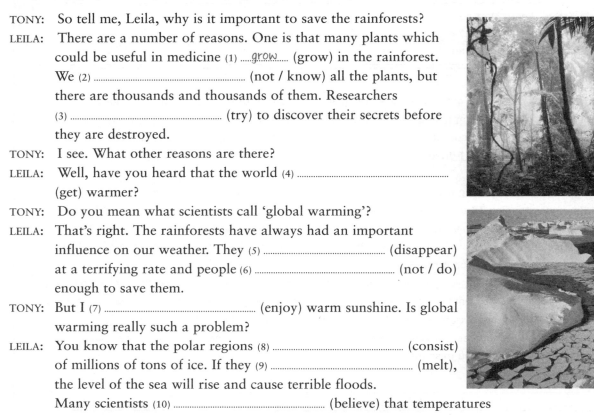

TONY: So tell me, Leila, why is it important to save the rainforests?

LEILA: There are a number of reasons. One is that many plants which
could be useful in medicine (1) ....grow.... (grow) in the rainforest.
We (2) .... (not / know) all the plants, but
there are thousands and thousands of them. Researchers
(3) .... (try) to discover their secrets before
they are destroyed.

TONY: I see. What other reasons are there?

LEILA: Well, have you heard that the world (4) ....
(get) warmer?

TONY: Do you mean what scientists call 'global warming'?

LEILA: That's right. The rainforests have always had an important
influence on our weather. They (5) .... (disappear)
at a terrifying rate and people (6) .... (not / do)
enough to save them.

TONY: But I (7) .... (enjoy) warm sunshine. Is global
warming really such a problem?

LEILA: You know that the polar regions (8) .... (consist)
of millions of tons of ice. If they (9) .... (melt),
the level of the sea will rise and cause terrible floods.
Many scientists (10) .... (believe) that temperatures
(11) .... (already / rise). We must do everything we can to prevent
global warming, and that includes preserving the rainforests!

TONY: Thank you, Leila, and good luck in your campaign.

LEILA: Thank you.

10   Tick (✓) the sentences which are correct. In some pairs, one sentence is correct. In other pairs, both sentences are correct.

1 What do you think of my hair? ✓	What are you thinking of my hair?
2 You look great today!	You're looking great today!
3 Do you enjoy your meal?	Are you enjoying your meal?
4 I think of selling my car. •	I'm thinking of selling my car.
5 Where do you live?	Where are you living?
6 I don't believe his story.	I'm not believing his story.
7 The students seem tired today.	The students are seeming tired today.
8 He weighs 80 kilos.	He's weighing 80 kilos.
9 How often do you play tennis?	How often are you playing tennis?
10 My brother looks for a new job.	My brother is looking for a new job.

Past simple and past continuous
(I did and I was doing)

11 Last week John went to Scotland on a business trip. Read his diary for last week. Then complete the report he wrote for his boss using the past simple.

6 MARCH	7 MARCH
Thursday	**Friday**
am fly to Edinburgh	am drive to Glasgow
have lunch with Scottish sales team	meet architect – look at new office plans
pm visit two factories	pm go to see new office building
discuss last series of adverts with	invite architect to dinner (not free)
marketing manager (not keen on them)	catch overnight train to London

Report: Visit to Scotland

Date: 6 & 7 March   Name: John Hutchings

I (1) ......flew...... to Edinburgh on Thursday morning and (2) .... lunch with
the Scottish sales team. Then I (3) .... our two factories there and
(4) .... our last series of adverts with the marketing manager.
He (5) .... keen on them, unfortunately.
    On Friday morning I (6) .... to Glasgow and (7) ....
the architect. We (8) .... at the new office plans and in the afternoon we
(9) .... to see the new office building. I (10) .... the
architect to dinner, but he (11) .... free. I (12) .... the
overnight train back to London.

12 Think about what you did one day last week. Complete the diary below. Then write a report using the past simple.

am	dinner
lunch	evening
pm	

Report:

Date: Name:

On .... morning I ....
....
....
....
....

13 Use the words given to make sentences. Do not change the order of the words. Use only the past simple or past continuous.

1

CATHY

We can't eat it because it's cold.

Cathy / phone / the restaurant when the pizza / arrive

...Cathy phoned the restaurant when the...
...pizza arrived....

2

Sorry I'm so late.

DON

when Don / arrive / we / have / coffee

...When Don arrived, we were having...
...coffee....

3

HENRY

while he / walk / in the mountains, Henry / see / a bear

....
....

4

the students / play / a game when the professor / arrive

....
....

5

Please send the fire brigade.

FELIX

Felix / phone / the fire brigade when the cooker / catch fire

....
....

6

when the starter / fire his pistol / the race / begin

....
....

7

I / walk / home when it / start / to snow

....
....

8

ANDY

Hi, Jenny!

Andy / come / out of the restaurant when he / see / Jenny

....
....

14 Choose the correct alternative.

Edison, Thomas Alva (1847–1931)
US inventor

Thomas Edison (1) <u>started</u> / ~~was starting~~ work on the railway when he was twelve, selling newspapers and snacks. There were long periods with nothing for him to do, so he (2) <u>built</u> / <u>was building</u> himself a little laboratory in the luggage van. He could carry out experiments there when he (3) <u>didn't sell</u> / <u>wasn't selling</u> things to passengers. He also (4) <u>joined</u> / <u>was joining</u> a library and (5) <u>read</u> / <u>was reading</u> every single book in it.

One day, when he (6) <u>waited</u> / <u>was waiting</u> at a station, he (7) <u>noticed</u> / <u>was noticing</u> a small boy. The boy (8) <u>played</u> / <u>was playing</u> by the track, unaware that a train (9) <u>approached</u> / <u>was approaching</u>. Edison (10) <u>ran</u> / <u>was running</u> out and (11) <u>grabbed</u> / <u>was grabbing</u> the child just in time. The child's father was so grateful that he (12) <u>offered</u> / <u>was offering</u> to teach

Edison to be a telegraph operator. Edison accepted the offer and soon he (13) <u>had</u> / <u>was having</u> regular lessons. After a year, he was good enough to get a job in the telegraph office. He continued to read and experiment whenever he (14) <u>had</u> / <u>was having</u> time. At twenty-one he (15) <u>left</u> / <u>was leaving</u> the telegraph office to devote all his time to being an inventor. He (16) <u>went on</u> / <u>was going on</u> to invent the electric light bulb, the phonograph and the movie camera.

15 Put the verbs into the correct form: past simple or past continuous.

My sister Naomi (1) ……met…… (meet) her husband when she (2) ……………………… (travel) round New Zealand. She and some friends (3) ……………………… (tour) the South Island when they (4) ……………………… (stop) in Christchurch for a few days. While her friends (5) ……………………… (shop), she (6) ……………………… (go) to look round an art gallery. She (7) ……………………… (look) at a sculpture when a young man (8) ……………………… (come) into the room and (9) ……………………… (start) to put it into his rucksack. She (10) ……………………… (call) the security guard because she (11) ……………………… (think) the young man (12) ……………………… (try) to steal it. She (13) ……………………… (be) very embarrassed to discover that the sculpture (14) ……………………… (belong) to the young man. However, while he (15) ……………………… (pack) it away, they (16) ……………………… (chat) and then he (17) ……………………… (ask) her to have a coffee with him. They (18) ……………………… (get married) three months later.

16 Here is part of the website of a rock star called Colin Boyle. Put the verbs into the correct form: past simple or past continuous.

Colin Boyle was born in 1983 near Dublin, Ireland. In 1996 he became seriously ill. While he (1) ...was recovering... (recover), his uncle (2) .... (give) him an old drumkit. He enjoyed playing and practised in a friend's garage every evening. One day in 1998, John Leaf, the manager of several successful musicians, (3) .... (pass) the garage when he (4) .... (hear) Colin practising. He (5) .... (bang) on the garage door and (6) .... (invite) Colin to appear in one of the concerts he (7) .... (organise) that year. Colin, however, (8) .... (refuse) Leaf's invitation, because at that time he (9) .... (prepare) for some important school exams.

Colin (10) .... (pass) his exams and (11) .... (go) to university to study engineering. At university he (12) .... (meet) Kim O'Malley, who (13) .... (study) chemistry. Kim played the saxophone. Being students, they rarely (14) .... (have) much money and they usually (15) .... (work) as waiters at weekends.

One evening in April 2001, while Colin and Kim (16) .... (serve) customers, the manager (17) .... (announce) that there would be no live music in the restaurant that night as the regular band could not come. Colin and Kim (18) .... (persuade) the manager to let them play. Everyone (19) .... (be) amazed to hear how good they (20) .... (be). In the next six months Colin and Kim (21) .... (earn) so much money they (22) .... (decide) to leave university and go on tour. Their success has continued ever since.

17 Complete the first sentence with the verb in the past continuous. Write a second sentence with the verb in the past simple to say what happened next. Use your own ideas.

1 When the phone rang, I ...was watching TV.
   ...I answered the phone.

2 I .... when it started to rain.

3 Everyone .... when the lights went out.

4 When we came out of the cinema, the sun ....

Present and past
(I do / I am doing and I did / I was doing)

18 Choose the correct alternative.

ADAM: Hello, Mike. What (1) <u>are you doing / ~~do you do~~</u> in this part of London?

MIKE: Well, actually, (2) <u>I'm looking / I look</u> at flats round here.

ADAM: Flats? (3) <u>Are you wanting / Do you want</u> to move?

MIKE: Yes. In fact, believe it or not, Mandy and I (4) <u>are getting / get</u> married.

ADAM: That's great! Congratulations. When (5) <u>were you deciding / did you decide</u>?

MIKE: Only last week. It was while we (6) <u>were staying / stayed</u> with her family in Scotland. Now (7) <u>we try / we're trying</u> to find a suitable flat.

ADAM: It'll be great to have you as neighbours. I hope you manage to buy one soon.

MIKE: Oh, we (8) <u>aren't looking / don't look</u> for one to buy. We (9) <u>aren't having / don't have</u> enough money yet. (10) <u>We're wanting / We want</u> to find somewhere to rent.

ADAM: Yes, of course. That's what Anna and I (11) <u>did / were doing</u> for six months. After that, my brother (12) <u>was lending / lent</u> us some money. That's how we (13) <u>were managing / managed</u> to buy ours.

MIKE: Really? Perhaps I'll talk to my family before (14) <u>we choose / we're choosing</u> a flat.

ADAM: That's not a bad idea. My family (15) <u>gave / were giving</u> us quite a lot of helpful advice. Now, have you got time for a coffee? There's a good place just round the corner.

MIKE: Yes, in fact I (16) <u>looked / was looking</u> for somewhere to have a snack when I bumped into you. Let's go.

19 Put the verbs into the correct form: present simple, present continuous, past simple or past continuous.

1 I remember the day you got your exam results. We ......<u>were watching</u>...... a film in the sitting-room when you rushed in and told us. (watch)

2 I tried to explain the situation to my parents, but they just .... what I was talking about. (not / understand)

3 What have you put in my burger? It .... absolutely disgusting. (taste)

4 Peter always claimed that he was innocent, but for many years no-one .... him. (believe)

5 It's a great jacket, I know, but unfortunately it .... to me. I'm just borrowing it for the party this evening. (not / belong)

6 Why .... that thin dress? You'll freeze to death in this cold wind! (you / wear)

7 Molly's fed up because she hurt her ankle when she .... this morning. (jog)

8 While I was admiring the view, someone stole the bag which .... all my traveller's cheques. (contain)

9 Look! .... that man standing beside the cash desk? I'm sure he's planning to steal something. (you / see)

10 Tea or coffee? I'm making both, so just say which you .... (prefer)

11 The boys didn't want to come shopping with us because they .... the football on television. (watch)

20 There are mistakes in eight of these sentences. Correct the sentences where necessary. Write 'OK' if the sentence is already correct.

1 The coffee is smelling wonderful.   *The coffee smells wonderful.*
2 Last year we visited Australia.   *OK*
3 The ship sank because the engineer wasn't calling for help until it was too late.
4 The reason I get fat is that I'm always tasting things while I'm cooking.
5 How is Jennifer? Does her health improve?
6 You're quite right, I'm completely agreeing with you.
7 What did you after you left school?
8 Now I understand what you're trying to say!
9 I can't imagine why you were believing all those stories.
10 Martin looked forward to a quiet evening when his brother came home from the football match with ten friends.
11 Philippa heard the election result as she was driving to work, so she phoned me when she got there.
12 I'm sorry, I've spilt your drink. Where are you keeping the paper towels?

21 Complete the email with suitable verbs in the correct form: present simple, present continuous, past simple or past continuous.

From: Alice Taylor
To: Anita Collins
Subject: Indian CDs

Dear Anita,

Thanks for the email, which (1) ...... *arrived* ...... yesterday. I (2) .... to feel much better now although my leg still (3) .... if I (4) .... too far.

Last weekend I (5) .... some friends who (6) .... the summer in a holiday house near here. I (7) .... to their house quite easily, but while I (8) .... home, my leg (9) .... to ache really badly. So this week I (10) .... more careful.

I'm very pleased you (11) .... to find that website about Indian music that you (12) .... for. I can lend you some CDs if you (13) ....

I must stop now because I (14) .... rather tired. Please email me again soon. I'm OK, but you know me, I (15) .... bored very quickly!

Love, Alice

22 Complete the questions with suitable verbs in the correct form: present simple, present continuous, past simple or past continuous.

1. Why *are you wearing* your coat and hat? — I'm really cold.

2. How often .... your teeth? — Twice a day.

3. When .... your driving test? — Last Friday. Would you like a lift somewhere?

4. .... this programme? — No, it's not very interesting.

5. What time .... to bed last night? — About one o'clock I think.

6. .... this jumper is too small for me? — Not at all. It's fine.

7. What .... at one o'clock this morning? — I was at home watching television.

8. What time .... ? — Nine o'clock, usually.

Present perfect simple and continuous
(I have done and I have been doing)

23 Complete the postcard with the present perfect simple form of the verbs.

Dear Fiona

As you can see from this postcard, I (1) ......**'ve arrived**...... (arrive) safely. Paul and I (2) **'ve already done** (already / do) lots of things even though I (3) **only have been** ...... (only / be) in New York twenty-four hours. I (4) **haven't slept** ...... (not sleep) for two days! I (5) **ve visited** ...... (visit) the Museum of Modern Art, I (6) **I've seen** ...... (see) a movie and I (7) **ve eaten** ...... (eat) a real American breakfast. I (8) **'ve ridden** ...... (ride) in a yellow cab and I (9) **'ve travelled** ...... (travel) on the subway too. I (10) **haven't spent** ...... (not / spend) any money yet because I (11) **haven't cashed** ...... (not / cash) any of my traveller's cheques. Paul (12) **has paid** ...... (pay) for everything so far.

I'll send you another card when I (13) **ve had** ...... (have) some sleep.

Love,

Theresa

24 Tick (✓) the sentence which means the same as the first sentence.

1 Have you ever visited Canada?
   a Did you visit Canada?
   b Have you been to Canada? ✓
   c Have you visited Canada recently?

2 This is the first time I've been skiing.
   a I've been skiing once before.
   b I haven't been skiing for a long time.
   c I've never been skiing before. ✓

3 I've had two holidays this year.
   a I've just come back from holiday.
   b I've been on holiday twice this year.
   c I've been away for two weeks.

4 We've just come home from the theatre.
   a We were at the theatre very recently.
   b We haven't been to the theatre for a long time.
   c We went to the theatre yesterday.

5 The manager hasn't been at work for a week.
   a The manager has left the company.
   b The manager has been away for a week.
   c The manager didn't come to work last week.

6 I haven't checked my emails since this morning.
   a I have just checked my emails.
   b I haven't checked my emails today.
   c I checked my emails this morning.

25 Complete the conversation with the verbs from the box in the correct form: present perfect simple or present perfect continuous. In some cases both forms are possible. You need to use some of the verbs more than once. Read the whole conversation before you begin.

be come do drive find have look

Jane is being interviewed by Mrs Carr for a job working with young children.

MRS CARR: Come in, Jane. Please sit down. Would you like a coffee?

JANE: Thank you, actually I (1) .....'ve just had.... (just) one.

MRS CARR: Oh good. Now, do you know this area at all?

JANE: Quite well. I've got friends who live in this town, so I (2) .... here for holidays since I was a child. I'm staying with them at the moment, actually.

MRS CARR: Oh, that's nice. And do you have a driving licence?

JANE: Yes. I (3) .... for four years now.

MRS CARR: And would you say you're a careful driver?

JANE: Yes, I think so. At least I (4) .... (never) an accident.

MRS CARR: Good. Now, could you tell me why you think you would be right for this job?

JANE: Well, I (5) .... (always) interested in working with small children. And I (6) .... two holiday jobs looking after children.

MRS CARR: How do you think you would cope in an emergency?

JANE: I'm quite a calm person, I think. I (7) .... a first aid course too. I got a certificate.

MRS CARR: That's good. Now, this job isn't permanent, as you know. We need someone for about a year. How would that fit with your long-term plans?

JANE: I'd like to work abroad eventually. But I want some full-time experience first. I (8) .... a Nursery Teacher's course this year. We finish next week, in fact.

MRS CARR: When would you be able to start?

JANE: As soon as I finish my course.

MRS CARR: Excellent. And would you live with your friends?

JANE: Well, probably not. I want to rent a small flat. I (9) .... in the paper every day, but I (10) .... (not) anything yet.

MRS CARR: Well, if you get the job, we'll try to help you. Now, would you like to come and meet some of the children?

JANE: Oh, yes.

MRS CARR: Right, if you'll just follow me then.

26 Tick (✓) the sentences which are correct. In some pairs, one sentence is correct. In other pairs, both sentences are correct.

1 She's had a headache all day. ✓   She's been having a headache all day.
2 I've wanted a dog for a long time.   I've been wanting a dog for a long time.
3 They've eaten lunch.   They've been eating lunch.
4 I've known her for two years.   I've been knowing her for two years.
5 He's been very helpful.   He's been being very helpful.
6 He's tasted the soup.   He's been tasting the soup.
7 They've seen this film before.   They've been seeing this film before.
8 I've seen a throat specialist   I've been seeing a throat specialist.
9 We've realised where we are now.   We've been realising where we are now.
10 It's belonged to us for many years.   It's been belonging to us for many years.
11 He's explained the plan to us.   He's been explaining the plan to us.
12 You've broken my pen.   You've been breaking my pen.

27 Put the verbs into the correct form: present perfect simple or present perfect continuous.

1 John's terribly upset. ......He's broken...... (he / break) off his engagement to Megan. Apparently ......she's been seeing.... (she / see) someone else while ...he's been... (he / be) in Africa.
2 Could you translate this Swedish newspaper article for me? I understood Swedish when I was a child, but .... (I / forget) it all.
3 What's that mark on the side of the car? .... (you / have) an accident?
4 This cassette recorder is broken. .... (you / play about) with it?
5 Your Italian is very good. .... (you / study) it long?
6 Of course you don't know what I think! .... (you / never / ask) my opinion.
7 I'm not surprised .... (he / fail) the exam. .... (he / not / work) hard recently.
8 Pete's hands are very dirty. .... (he / repair) the garden wall.
9 I'm going to give that cat some food. .... (it / sit) on the doorstep for hours. I'm sure it's starving.
10 .... (I / do) grammar exercises all morning. I deserve a treat for lunch.
11 Where are my keys? This is the third time .... (I / lose) them today!
12 Oh, do be quiet. .... (you / grumble) all day!
13 Since Maria won the lottery .... (she / spend) money like water. .... (she / buy) a new car and .... (she / move) to a big new house. .... (she / give) wonderful parties every weekend too. In fact, I'm going to one tomorrow.

28 Complete the sentences with the verbs in the correct form: present perfect simple or present perfect continuous.

1 *earlier this morning* — *now*

You look very tired.

Yes, I am. I've been doing an exam all morning.

2 *about now* — *now*

ARRIVALS ↑

WELCOME TO NEW YORK

Isn't your brother here?

Sorry, no. He ....

3 *earlier today* — *now*

You're looking very smart

Thanks, I ....

4 *a few minutes ago* — *now*

Why are you crying?

Don't worry. It's because I ....

5 *earlier this week* — *now*

FOR SALE

Can you give me a lift to work?

I'm afraid I can't. You see, I ....

6 *a moment ago* — *now*

Why do you want a plaster?

Because I ....

7 *earlier this afternoon* — *now*

How did you get in such a mess?

Well, I .... with my friends.

8 *earlier this year* — *now*

DANCING SCHOOL

You dance much better than you used to!

Thank you. Actually, I ....

Present perfect simple and continuous; past simple
(I have done and I have been doing; I did)

29 Complete the second sentence so that it has a similar meaning to the first sentence.

1 We haven't been to a concert for over a year.
The last time we ....*went to a concert*.... was over a year ago.

2 Your birthday party was the last time I really enjoyed myself.
I .... since your birthday party.

3 It's nearly twenty years since my father saw his brother.
My father .... for nearly twenty years.

4 James went to Scotland last Friday and is still there.
James has .... to Scotland.

5 When did you learn to drive?
How long is it .... to drive?

6 The last time I went swimming was when we were in Spain.
I haven't .... we were in Spain.

7 You haven't tidied this room for weeks.
It's weeks .... this room.

8 We started looking for a flat two months ago and we're still looking.
We've .... a flat for two months.

9 This is the first time I've been to a nightclub.
I .... to a nightclub before.

10 Kim lost her job a year ago.
Kim .... a job for the last year.

30 Use your own ideas to complete the sentences. Use the present perfect simple, the present perfect continuous or the past simple.

1 Since we moved house, ...*we've had lots of visitors*....................... .
                or ...*we've been having lots of visitors*................ .

2 ...*I was ill, so I didn't go to work*................................. last week.

3 .... for several years.

4 .... since yesterday.

5 When I was a child, ...

6 .... ten minutes ago.

7 It's three weeks since ....

8 For the past three weeks ....

9 .... in 2001.

10 .... since I came into this room.

11 Last December ....

12 .... since I got up this morning.

Present perfect and present
(I have done / I have been doing and I do / I am doing)

31 Choose the correct alternative.

Megan meets her friend Jess in an Internet café.

MEGAN: Hi, Jess, how are you? (1) <u>I haven't seen</u> / ~~I haven't been seeing~~ you since the summer.

JESS: No, (2) <u>I've been revising</u> / <u>I've revised</u> for my exams. They're next week. What about you?

MEGAN: Well, last week I met a website designer, Steve, (3) <u>who's looking</u> / <u>who's been looking</u> for an assistant for weeks. (4) <u>He offers</u> / <u>He's offered</u> me some work.

JESS: That's great.

MEGAN: Yeah, so every day since then (5) <u>I look</u> / <u>I've been looking</u> at his work online.
(6) <u>He's designed</u> / <u>He's been designing</u> three or four really cool sites already. But
(7) <u>he doesn't have</u> / <u>he isn't having</u> enough time to do everything. That's why
(8) <u>he's needing</u> / <u>he needs</u> me.

JESS: That's really good. Hey, who's that guy over there? (9) <u>He's looked</u> / <u>He's been looking</u> at us since we came in.

MEGAN: Oh, that's Steve, the designer (10) <u>I've been telling</u> / <u>I tell</u> you about.

JESS: (11) <u>He's looking</u> / <u>He looks</u> like a student or something, not a businessman.

MEGAN: Shh. (12) <u>He's coming</u> / <u>He comes</u> this way.

STEVE: Hi, Megan.

MEGAN: Steve, this is my friend Jess.

STEVE: Hello. (13) <u>Do you spend</u> / <u>Are you spending</u> the afternoon here?

JESS: That's right. (14) <u>I come</u> / <u>I'm coming</u> here most days after lunch. (15) <u>I'm</u> / <u>I've been</u> here since one o'clock today.

STEVE: (16) <u>Do you enjoy</u> / <u>Are you enjoying</u> yourself?

JESS: Er, yes. Thank you. But why?

STEVE: Oh, just interested. (17) <u>I own</u> / <u>I'm owning</u> this café.

19

32 Complete the sentences with the verbs from the box in the correct form: present perfect simple, present perfect continuous, present simple or present continuous.

not / be	~~deal~~	~~not / finish~~	have	not / know	live	see	not / see
not / speak	stare	stay	suffer	wait	not / want	watch	

1 I ...haven't finished... checking the emails because I ...'ve been dealing... with customers all morning.

2 Thank you, but I really .... any more juice. I .... two large glasses already.

3 Paul .... from earache since the weekend. He .... the doctor twice, but it's still not better.

4 We .... why Sara is upset, but she .... to us for ages.

5 Why .... you .... at me like that? I suppose you .... a woman on a motorbike before!

6 I .... with my cousin in London for a few days. I .... here before, but he .... here for several years, so he can show me around.

7 I'm sorry I'm late. .... you .... a long time?

8 We .... this stupid film since lunchtime. Let's switch over to the other channel.

33 Complete the postcard with suitable verbs in the correct form: present perfect simple, present perfect continuous, present simple or present continuous.

Dear Nick,
We (1) ...are having... a wonderful time here in York. We (2) ....
here for three days now and we (3) .... to stay for the rest
of the week because we (4) .... ourselves so much. We
(5) .... the Cathedral and the Castle Museum, and this morning
we (6) .... around the little old-fashioned streets, looking at the
shops and cafés. I (7) .... this postcard just before lunch. We
(8) .... any souvenirs yet, but we (9) ....
some good long walks in the countryside, which is beautiful. Fortunately,
the weather (10) .... very good so far.
People (11) .... it can be very cold and it
often (12) .... for days! As this is the
first time we (13) .... to England, we
(14) .... that we're just lucky.
See you soon,
Roberto and Jan

34 Put the verbs into the correct form: present perfect simple, present perfect continuous, present simple or present continuous.

Sam is the captain of his local football team. He's talking to his brother, Dave.

SAM: Dave, I'm worried about the team.

DAVE: But why? (1) ....._You've won_..... (You / win) every game this season.

SAM: Yeah, (2) .... (we / be) very lucky. That's

        (3) .... (what / cause) me problems now.

DAVE: How come?

SAM: Well, (4) .... (we / practise) twice a week this season and

        (5) .... (that / really / make) a difference. Now, some of the guys

        say that's not necessary because (6) .... (we / always / win).

        I'm afraid that if (7) .... (we / not / practise) so often, we

        may lose our matches. (8) .... (We / play) Donnington on

        Saturday and (9) .... (everyone / agree) they're a really strong

        team. The trouble is, (10) .... (we / not / practise) since Monday.

DAVE: I can see (11) .... (you / have) a problem. What can you do?

SAM: I think the problem is really Colin.

DAVE: The big guy (12) .... (who / play) for you since last season?

SAM: Yes. (13) .... (He / usually / score) most of our goals.

        Since the summer (14) .... (he / arrive) for training really

        late. When I try to talk to him, (15) .... (he / refuse) to

        listen to what (16) .... (I / say).

DAVE: Well, tell him he can't play if (17) .... (he / not / listen) to you.

SAM: I guess I'll have to. (18) .... (I / not / like) it. What if he

        gets angry and leaves the team?

DAVE: I'm sure he won't.

SAM: (19) .... (I / hope) not.

21

Present perfect, present and past
(I have done / I have been doing, I do / I am doing and I did)

35 There are seven mistakes in this letter. Correct the mistakes.

Dear Mr Aziz,

I would like to apply for the job of shop manager which ~~I see~~ <u>I have seen</u> advertised in the local paper.

I am twenty years old. I was born in France, but my family moved to England when I was twelve and I am living here ever since. I left school since three years and since then I am having several jobs in shops. For the past six months I am working in Halls Department Store. The manager has been saying that he is willing to give me a reference.

I speak French and English fluently. I have also learnt German since I left school, so I speak some German too.

I hope you will consider my application.

Yours sincerely,

Louise Brett

36 Write an application letter for this job. You may write for yourself or you may invent an applicant.

> Bright, helpful person required to help for two months in souvenir shop this summer. Must speak some English in addition to at least one other language. Experience and qualifications not essential, but desirable. Excellent pay and conditions. Write, giving details + one referee, to:
> Ms J. Sparks, The Old Shop, High St, Allingham DE3 2GJ.

....
....
....
....
....
....
....
....
....

Present perfect and past simple
(I have done / I have been doing and I did)

37 Match the beginning of each sentence with the most suitable ending to make a story.

1	The Ocean Hotel opened	*a*	half an hour ago.	1	....c....
2	There's been a nightclub there	*b*	last night.	2	....
3	I went clubbing there	~~*c* in the 1990s.~~		3	....
4	I lost my coat	*d*	since January.	4	....
5	I phoned the club	*e*	all day.	5	....
6	The manager asked me to wait	*f*	when I went there.	6	....
7	That's why I've felt cold	*g*	for a few days in case it's found.	7	....

38 Choose the correct alternative.

1 My sister <u>has been / ~~was~~</u> interested in medicine ever since she <u>~~has been~~ / was</u> a child.

2 How long <u>have you studied / did you study</u> before you <u>have qualified / qualified</u>?

3 Where <u>have you first met / did you first meet</u> your boyfriend?

4 Is this the first time <u>you've cooked / you cooked</u> pasta?

5 We <u>have wanted / wanted</u> to go to the cinema last night, but there <u>haven't been / weren't</u> any seats.

6 What can we do? I'm sure something <u>has happened / happened</u> to Alex. <u>We've been waiting / We waited</u> over an hour and <u>he hasn't phoned / he hasn't been phoning</u> yet.

7 <u>I've posted / I posted</u> that CD to you three weeks ago. If you still <u>haven't received / didn't receive</u> it, please email me immediately.

8 I'm exhausted because <u>I've worked / I've been working</u> in a restaurant for the past three weeks. <u>I've never realised / I never realised</u> how hard it is!

39 Complete the sentences with the verbs from the box in the correct form: present perfect or past simple.

~~be~~ be break earn forget give go have offer open speak tell

1 Bill ....*has been*.... away from school all this week.

2 Glenda .... to the cinema every weekend when she was a student.

3 Pippa .... very quiet recently. Is she OK?

4 Eric .... the door before I rang the bell.

5 How long .... Neil .... his present job?

6 .... Tina .... to her parents since she left home?

7 Ow, that hurt! I think I .... my toe.

8 Jock .... me about his problems last night.

9 I .... Sue's mobile number. Do you have it?

10 Jane .... more money in her last job, but she enjoys this one more.

11 .... Brian .... you his new address before he moved house?

12 My brother .... to lend me his car tomorrow, so I needn't get the bus.

40 Put the verbs into the correct form: present perfect simple or past simple.

THEN and NOW

Twenty-five years ago few people (1) ....*realised*.... (realise) that computers were about to become part of our daily lives. This short period of time (2) .... (see) enormous changes, in business, education and public administration. Jobs which (3) .... (take) weeks to complete in the past are now carried out in minutes. People who (4) .... (spend) all day copying and checking calculations are now freed from these boring tasks. Students (5) .... (become) as familiar with hardware and software as their parents (6) .... (be) with pencils and exercise books. Computerisation of public records (7) .... (enable) government departments to analyse the needs of citizens in detail.

Some of us may wonder, however, whether life (8) .... (really / improve) as a result of these changes. Many jobs (9) .... (disappear), for example, when intelligent machines (10) .... (take) over the work. Employers complain that clerical staff (11) .... (become) dependent on calculators and cannot do simple arithmetic. There are fears that governments (12) .... (not / do) enough to ensure that personal information held on computers is really kept secret. Certainly, many people may now be wondering whether the spread of computers (13) .... (bring) us as many problems as it (14) .... (solve).

41 Alex wants to go to an art college and is being interviewed by Tom Smith, one of the lecturers. Complete the questions which Tom asks him. Read the whole conversation before you begin.

TOM: Right, Alex, let's find out something about you. When (1) ....*did you leave*.... school?

ALEX: Five years ago, actually.

TOM: And where (2) .... since then?

ALEX: Well, I've had several jobs.

TOM: What (3) .... first?

ALEX: I worked in a café for about a year. I needed to save a lot of money.

TOM: Why (4) .... the money?

ALEX: I wanted to travel a bit before I started studying.

TOM: Where (5) .... to go?

ALEX: Well, the Middle East, Latin America, Australia …

TOM: Wow! And (6) .... all those places?

ALEX: No, not yet. I've been to Brazil and Peru so far. And I spent some months in Turkey.

TOM: Where (7) .... there?

ALEX: With some friends near Izmir. It was great.

TOM: You're very lucky. And now you want to come to college.

(8) .... some work to show me?

ALEX: Um, yes, I've got some paintings here.

TOM: Where (9) .... these?

ALEX: Mostly in Turkey.

TOM: (10) .... anything in South America?

ALEX: No, I didn't have time really. And I was travelling light, so I just did some pencil sketches. They're behind the paintings.

TOM: Well, Alex, I'm very impressed. When (11) .... interested in painting and drawing?

ALEX: I think I always have been.

TOM: I can believe that. This work is very good.

ALEX: Thank you very much.

42 Choose ten of the pictures and write true sentences about yourself. Use the present perfect or past simple.

drive / car	play / volleyball	ride / bicycle	study / English	eat / burger
play / tennis	do / washing up	watch / television	suck / thumb	eat / birthday cake
get / married	break / leg	pass / exam	write / email	ride / motorbike

1 I *haven't eaten a burger* .... since last month.

2 Yesterday I ....

3 In the past six months I ....

4 Since my last birthday I ....

5 I .... recently.

6 Last year I ....

7 Six months ago I ....

8 I .... when I was a child.

9 I .... yesterday evening.

10 This week I ....

Past simple, past continuous and past perfect
(I did, I was doing and I had done / I had been doing)

43 Choose the correct alternative.

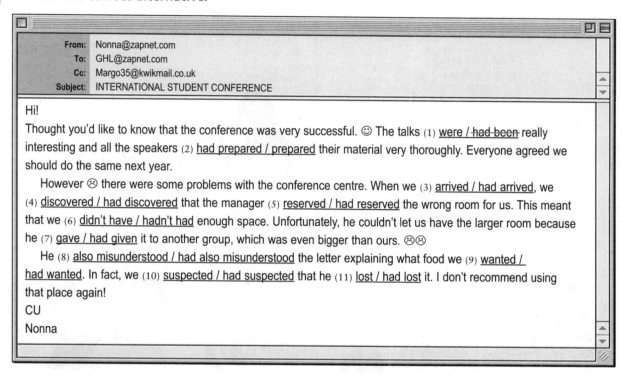

From: Nonna@zapnet.com
To: GHL@zapnet.com
Cc: Margo35@kwikmail.co.uk
Subject: INTERNATIONAL STUDENT CONFERENCE

Hi!

Thought you'd like to know that the conference was very successful. ☺ The talks (1) <u>were / had been</u> really interesting and all the speakers (2) <u>had prepared / prepared</u> their material very thoroughly. Everyone agreed we should do the same next year.

However ☹ there were some problems with the conference centre. When we (3) <u>arrived / had arrived</u>, we (4) <u>discovered / had discovered</u> that the manager (5) <u>reserved / had reserved</u> the wrong room for us. This meant that we (6) <u>didn't have / hadn't had</u> enough space. Unfortunately, he couldn't let us have the larger room because he (7) <u>gave / had given</u> it to another group, which was even bigger than ours. ☹☹

He (8) <u>also misunderstood / had also misunderstood</u> the letter explaining what food we (9) <u>wanted / had wanted</u>. In fact, we (10) <u>suspected / had suspected</u> that he (11) <u>lost / had lost</u> it. I don't recommend using that place again!

CU

Nonna

44 There are mistakes in all of these sentences. Correct the sentences.

1 I was pleased to see my old college friends at the conference last week <u>as we didn't see each other</u> since we finished our course.

as we hadn't seen each other ....

2 By the time we reached the theatre, the play ended and the audience was leaving.

....

3 At the end of their meal, they found they couldn't pay the bill because they didn't bring any money with them.

....

4 We were pleased that Gary was having his laptop with him, but we were less pleased when we discovered that he hadn't charged the battery.

....

5 When I came out of the cinema, I had found that a thief had taken my car radio.

....

6 At first the authorities thought the athlete had been taking drugs, but they soon realised they mixed up the results of the tests.

....

7 When my cousin came into the room, I didn't recognise her because I didn't see her since she was a little girl.

....

8 We couldn't find a parking space when we reached the city centre, so we had decided to go by bus the next time.

....

45 Complete the sentences with suitable verbs in the correct form: past perfect simple or past perfect continuous.

1

MAGGIE

Why did Maggie take a shower?

Because *she'd been playing tennis* .

2

REBECCA

Why did Rebecca buy a new car?

Because she ....
....

3

JORDAN

Why didn't Jordan answer the door?

Because he ....
....

4

BRUCE

Why did Bruce go to hospital?

Because he ....
....

5

ALEX

Why didn't Alex eat any lunch?

Because she ....
....

6

CORA

Why did Cora miss the bus?

Because she ....
....

7

JILL

Why didn't Jill go for a walk?

Because she ....
....

8

CHRIS

Why did Chris lose his job?

Because he ....
....

46 Put the verbs into the correct form: past simple, past continuous, past perfect simple or past perfect continuous.

Kylie has called to see her boyfriend Gary. They are both angry.

GARY: Kylie, I'm surprised to see you.

KYLIE: Yeah? Well, I think you owe me an explanation.

GARY: What about you? (1) .....I...saw..... (I / see) you in the café last night. (2) .... (We / arrange) to meet at the cinema, if you remember.

KYLIE: So why (3) .... (you / not / come) into the café if you saw me?

GARY: (4) .... (I / be) too angry. And cold. (5) .... (I / wait) outside the cinema for three-quarters of an hour.

KYLIE: But why? (6) .... (you / not / get) my note?

GARY: What note?

KYLIE: The note (7) .... (I / leave) here yesterday afternoon.

GARY: What are you taking about?

KYLIE: (8) .... (I / go) past the cinema yesterday lunchtime when (9) .... (I / notice) that (10) .... (they / change) the film. So (11) .... (I / put) a note under your door to tell you.

GARY: (12) .... (I / not / find) a note.

KYLIE: It must be here. Let me look. Yes, it's here, under the mat.

GARY: Oh, right. I'm sorry I was angry. It's just that, well, while (13) .... (I / wait), (14) .... (I / worry) about (15) .... (what / happen) to you. Then (16) .... (I / see) you in the café. (17) .... (You / laugh) with your friends and (18) .... (I / realise) that (19) .... (you / sit) there in the warm with them all evening. That's why (20) .... (I / lose) my temper.

KYLIE: Never mind. Let's forget it. Where shall we go now?

GARY: What's on at the cinema, then?

KYLIE: A new musical. (21) .... (My sister / see) it yesterday. (22) .... (She / sing) the theme song all morning.

GARY: Oh, you must be tired of hearing it.

KYLIE: I am. Let's just go and have something to eat, shall we?

GARY: Yes, that's a good idea.

Past simple, past continuous and used to
(I did, I was doing and I used to do)

---

47 Write sentences with **used to** or **didn't use to**.

1 I had a lot of money, but I lost it all when my business failed.
   I used to be rich.

2 I quite like jazz now, although I wasn't keen on it when I was younger.

3 I seem to have lost interest in my work.

4 My sister has put on a lot of weight.

5 Now that I can afford First Class, I don't mind air travel.

6 My brother had his hair cut short when he left college.

7 I gave up smoking five years ago.

8 My parents lived in Africa before I was born.

9 When he was younger, my uncle was a swimming champion.

10 Since we moved to the countryside, we've bought a car.

---

48 Choose the correct alternative.

I t is sometimes said that there is nothing new in the world of fashion. Annabelle was a well-known model during the seventies. When her children were in their early teens, they (1) <u>were enjoying</u> / <u>used to enjoy</u> looking at her old photo albums. They (2) <u>were finding</u> / <u>found</u> it hard to believe that she (3) <u>was wearing</u> / <u>used to wear</u> such strange clothes. (4) <u>Did people really use to think</u> / <u>Were people really thinking</u> flared trousers looked good? And those ugly platform shoes! Annabelle (5) <u>was admitting</u> / <u>admitted</u> that people (6) <u>were often falling</u> / <u>often used to fall</u> over because their heels were so high. When her children grew up, however, Annabelle noticed to her amusement that seventies styles (7) <u>were</u> / <u>used to be</u> in fashion again. 'I (8) <u>planned</u> / <u>was planning</u> to throw all my old clothes away,' she said, 'but my daughter went to a party last week, and guess what she (9) <u>used to wear</u> / <u>was wearing</u> – that's right, some of my old clothes!'

49 Underline the verbs which can be changed to **used to** (used to work / used to play / used to be, etc.) instead of the past simple. If no change is possible, write 'No change'. Rewrite the sentences with **used to** where possible.

1 Every summer, Eileen <u>worked</u> in a café while her friends were on holiday.
   Every summer, Eileen used to work in a café while her friends were on holiday.

2 Bruce drove his new car to Scotland, stopping one night in the north of England.
   No change

3 My girlfriend had a dog which she had rescued from drowning when it was a puppy.

4 As Mary was getting out of the boat, her foot slipped and she fell into the river.

5 Before the new shopping centre was built, there was a football pitch here.

6 Jasper complained that bread didn't taste like cardboard until the supermarkets started making it.

7 During our trip to the Antarctic I took lots of photos of the seabirds which followed the ship.

8 While I was waiting for the bus, I noticed a group of tourists who were listening to a guide.

9 The music in this club was very boring before the new disc jockey came to work here.

10 I spent a lot of time helping round the house when I was a kid, but my sister didn't help at all.

11 The politicians made lots of promises before the election but kept none of them, as usual.

50 Write true sentences about yourself with **used to** or **didn't use to** and the words from the box.

cinema   friends   grandparents   homework
jeans   music   restaurants   television

1 *I used to go on holiday with my parents, but now I go with my friends.*
2 *I didn't use to wear jeans when I was a child.*
3
4
5
6
7
8

31

51 Complete the sentences with suitable verbs in the correct form: past simple, past continuous or **used to**.

1 When did Ellie meet her boyfriend?

ELLIE

I think it was while she ....was studying.... in the States.

2 Why does Warren keep shouting at people?

I don't know. He .... so bad-tempered.

WARREN

3 How long is it since you .... a holiday?

Not since last year.

4 CLUB COSTA

Is the club shut already?

Yeah, it .... open much later than it does now.

5 Did I hear you on the phone earlier?

Oh, yes. I .... to the bank manager.

6 Have you ever ridden a motorbike?

Yes, once. But I .... off at a roundabout.

7 I didn't know you understood Italian!

Oh, I .... it while I .... in Rome.

8 How do you know London so well?

Well, I .... here.

52 Choose the correct alternative.

A PETE: What part of Birmingham (1) do you live / did you live / have you lived in when you
              (2) were / have been / were being a child?

   PATRICK: A place called Selly Oak. (3) Do you know / Did you know / Have you known it?

   PETE: Oh, yes. I (4) was cycling / used to cycle / have cycled through it nearly every day
              when I (5) was studying / have been studying / have studied there.

B HELEN: When (6) are you hearing / did you hear / have you heard the result of your law
              exam?

   CLARA: When I (7) phoned / have phoned / had phoned my boss. She (8) is checking /
              has been checking / was checking the list when I (9) had rung / rang / was ringing, so
              she (10) has told / was telling / told me then.

   HELEN: (11) Do you expect / Have you expected / Had you been expecting to do so well?

   CLARA: Not really, to be honest!

   HELEN: (12) Are you emailing / Do you email / Have you emailed your husband yet?

   CLARA: Not yet.

   HELEN: Go on! He (13) waited / has waited / has been waiting to hear from you all day.

53 Put the verbs into the correct form: present simple, present continuous, past simple, past
continuous, present perfect simple, present perfect continuous or past perfect simple.

1 Tom has had to give up playing football since he ....broke.... (break) his ankle.

2 How often .... (you / visit) your cousins when you
   .... (you / be) in the States last year?

3 I .... (not pay) you for my ticket yet. How much .... (I /
   owe) you?

4 The hotel manager called the police when he .... (discover) that a guest
   .... (leave) without paying his bill.

5 Sharon's work is terrible these days. I don't know what .... (happen) to
   her. She .... (lose) interest in everything recently.

6 We .... (have) a fire in the office last week. We ....
   (sort) out the mess ever since, as you can imagine.

7 My grandmother was a wonderful woman. She .... (spend) most of her
   life teaching adults who .... (miss) the opportunity to go to school when
   they .... (be) children.

8 I .... (always / want) to visit Japan. Now that I .... (have)
   the chance, I .... (decide) to take it.

9 We .... (go) to the theatre early, but a lot of people
   .... (arrive) before us and there .... (be) a long
   queue for tickets.

10 My sister's in Australia at the moment. She .... (have) a wonderful time
   there.

54 Choose the correct alternative.

A BEN: Are you busy at the moment, Sam?

SAM: Yes. (1) I prepare / I'm preparing for a conference next Wednesday, but
(2) that only lasts / that is only lasting until Friday so I'm free at the weekend.

B PAT: Oh dear, I've spilt my coffee.

ALAN: Don't worry! (3) I get / I'll get a cloth.

C WILL: What time (4) does your evening class finish / is your evening class finishing?

LIZ: Half past nine.

WILL: (5) Shall I come / Do I come and collect you?

LIZ: Thanks, but (6) I meet / I'm meeting my sister for a drink.

D MIKE: Mum, (7) will you talk / are you talking to Dad for me?

MUM: What's the problem?

MIKE: Last week he said I could use the car at the weekend, but now (8) he doesn't let /
he won't let me after all. I need it to get to the match (9) I play / I'm playing on Sunday.

MUM: OK. (10) I try / I'll try to make him change his mind. I expect (11) he's agreeing /
he'll agree when I explain.

55 Complete the note with the verbs from the box in the correct form: present simple, present
continuous or the will/shall future.

| be come ~~go~~ include let see work |

Hi, Mike

I've had an idea about next year's holiday. I (1) .....'m going.....
to the States on a tour, starting on 10th July. Would you like
to come with me? I know you (2) .... in
Japan next summer, but I'm sure your company
(3) .... you fly to the States instead of
coming back to Europe. The tour (4) ....
New York, Boston, Philadelphia and Washington (see the enclosed
brochure) and there (5) .... chances to
visit other places too. What do you think? Let me know quickly
because I (6) .... the travel agent on
Monday. I really hope you (7) ....

All the best

Pete

Tour the
UNITED STATES
in air-conditioned luxury

56 Put the verbs into the correct form: present simple, present continuous or the **will/shall** future.

Greg and Brian are going to an international students' conference. Greg's checking with Brian about the arrangements he's made for them.

GREG: Is everything arranged for tomorrow? What time (1) _does our plane leave_ (our plane / leave)?

BRIAN: At eight-thirty, so (2) .... (I / collect) you from your house at six.

GREG: Six! (3) .... (I / have to) get up in the middle of the night.

BRIAN: I'm sorry, but we must check in by seven and I think (4) .... (there / probably / be) a long queue.

GREG: Oh, OK. What about the other end?

BRIAN: Well, (5) .... (a local student / come) to the airport to meet us. I spoke to him this morning.

GREG: That's good. (6) .... (We / be able to) talk on the way to the hostel.

BRIAN: Right. I believe (7) .... (the conference / not start) until noon. Anyway, (8) .... (they / email) a programme to us before we leave.

GREG: Great. (9) .... (I / read) it on the plane, I expect. Now, I'd better go and pack.

BRIAN: Yeah, me too. See you tomorrow at six.

GREG: Oh, yeah. I hope (10) .... (I / be) awake.

BRIAN: So do I.

57 Complete the following sentences about yourself using the words in brackets.

1 This lesson _ends at twelve o'clock_ . (end)
2 At the weekend _I'll probably go to the cinema_ . (probably go)
3 Next summer .... (visit)
4 When I finish this exercise, ... (be)
5 Tomorrow evening I expect .... (eat)
6 At the end of my course .... (probably speak)
7 My next class .... (begin)
8 Next week .... (have)
9 My course .... (finish)

58 Imagine that you are in the following situations. Write what you say using **will**, **shall** or **won't**.

1

YOU

You offer to help her.
You say: *I'll take the briefcase for you.*
or *Shall I carry something?*

2

Don't be late.

YOU

You promise not to be late.
You say: ....

3

Can you deliver before the weekend?

YOU

You agree to deliver the goods on Friday.
You say: ....

4

YOU

We haven't got anything to do.

You suggest going to the swimming pool.
You say: ....

5

YOU

You ask them to stop fighting.
You say: ....

6

YOU

You explain the problem with the door.
You say: ....

7

YOU

You offer to phone for an ambulance.
You say: ....

8

YOU

You refuse to pay for the goods until you've
checked that they aren't damaged.
You say: ....
....

The future: present continuous, will/shall, going to
(I am doing, I will/shall do, I am going to do)

59 Write sentences with **going to** and the words in brackets.

1 It's Rowland's birthday next week. (send him a card)
 I'm going to send him a card.

2 Look at those dark clouds. (rain very soon)

3 John forgot his wedding anniversary. (be in trouble)

4 This room is a mess. (who / help me tidy up?)

5 Alex and Tony can't afford to stay in a hotel. (buy a tent)

6 This fish tastes horrible. (not come to this restaurant again)

7 I need to get more exercise. (walk to work from now on)

8 I'm very tired this evening. (have an early night)

9 We haven't got any money. (how / get home?)

10 I need to use the car early tomorrow morning. (buy petrol tonight)

11 My parents dislike flying. (travel to Prague by train)

12 Leila's lost her CD player. (buy a new one?)

60 Choose the correct alternative.

1 The sports club has put up the prices again. I'll cancel / I'm going to cancel my membership.
2 I've talked to my boss, but he's very unhelpful and won't do / isn't going to do anything about the problem.
3 I'll go / I'm going to go into town this afternoon. Can I get you anything?
4 Will you hold / Are you going to hold this box for a moment while I unpack it?
5 I hear the government's announced they'll raise / they're going to raise taxes again.
6 My car won't start / isn't going to start. It must be the cold, I think.
7 I'll start / I'm going to start a new job next week.
8 I'm so sorry I forgot your birthday. Why don't you come round tomorrow evening and I'll cook / I'm going to cook you a meal?
9 I took these trousers back to the shop, but they won't change / they aren't going to change them without a receipt.
10 You look tired. Shall we eat / Are we going to eat early this evening?
11 John's sold his car. He'll buy / He's going to buy a bike, he says.
12 I've decided what to do for my holiday. I'll go / I'm going to go to Morocco.

61 Put the verbs into the correct form: the **will/shall** future or the **going** to future.

Mary and Nigel run a shop together. They are having money problems.

Monday

MARY: I don't know what (1) ...*we're going to do*... (we / do).
We've hardly made any money for ages.

NIGEL: I think we should advertise. We can send out leaflets.

MARY: Yes. (2) ...*That will probably get*... (That / probably /
get) our name more widely known. But do you think
(3) .... (people /
come) into the shop?

NIGEL: Well, we could try advertising in the local paper.

MARY: That might be better.
(4) .... (I / phone) and
find out their rates. And what about local radio?

NIGEL: Good idea. (5) .... (I / phone) them?

MARY: OK, thanks.

Tuesday

MARY: We haven't got enough money to pay for all the
advertising we need. I've been in touch with the bank.
(6) .... (I / see) the
manager on Friday.

NIGEL: (7) .... (he / give)
us a loan, do you think?

MARY: I hope so.

Friday

MANAGER: So you want to borrow some money. How do you want
to spend it?

MARY: (8) .... (We / advertise) on local radio
and in the paper. We've planned it carefully. We only need
£2,000.

MANAGER: Very well. (9) ....
(The bank / lend) you the money. But you must
pay us back in three months. Can you do that?

MARY: (10) ....
(We / do) it, I promise.

MANAGER: Now, go and see the loans clerk and
(11) ....
(he / help) you fill in the necessary forms.

MARY: Thank you for your help.

MANAGER: You're welcome.

62 Complete the conversations.

A ANN: It just said on the radio that (1) ___it's going to snow___ .

   BILL: Oh, did it? I (2) ___'ll take___ my big coat then.

   JOE: Good idea. So (3) _____ . Come on, Bill. Let's go.

B ED: Jenny's had her baby.

   GAIL: Really? That's wonderful! (4) _____ her some flowers.

   ED: (5) _____ her this afternoon at the hospital.

   (6) _____ them to her for you if you want.

   GAIL: (7) _____ you? Thanks very much. In that case,

   (8) _____ and buy them right away.

C KEN: I haven't got a clean shirt. (9) _____ one for me?

   LILY: No, (10) _____ . You can do your own washing!

63 Write what you would say in these situations. Use **will/shall, going to** or the present continuous.

1 You make your friend a cup of sweet coffee, then she tells you she doesn't take sugar. Offer to make her another one.
   You: ___·I'm sorry, I'll make you another one.___

2 A colleague asks why you're leaving work early. Explain that you have a doctor's appointment.
   You: _____

3 Your brother lent you some money last week. Promise to pay him back at the weekend.
   You: _____

4 Your sister has bought some CDs very cheap. You want to get some too and you've asked her several times where she got them, but she refuses to tell you. Ask why she refuses to tell you.
   You: _____ ?

5 You failed an exam last year. Since then you've been working hard. Tell your teacher it's because you're determined not to fail again.
   You: _____

6 Your neighbour is playing loud music late at night. You get angry and ask him to turn the volume down.
   You: _____ ?

7 You've been offered a role in a film and have accepted. Tell your friends about it.
   You: _____ !

8 A friend is telling you about her wedding plans. Ask her where they plan to go for their honeymoon.
   You: _____

64 Put the verbs into the correct form: present simple, present continuous, the **will/shall** future, the **going to** future, the future continuous or the future perfect.

A Mick is watching television when his sister Vanessa comes into the room.

MICK: What are you doing in your dressing-gown? It's only eight o'clock.

VANESSA: I don't feel well. (1) ....*I'm going to have*.... (I / have) an early night.

MICK: Oh, dear. I hope (2) ....*you feel*.... (you / feel) better in the morning.

VANESSA: So do I. (3) .... (I / meet) my new boss at ten o'clock.

MICK: I think (4) .... (I / make) some tea when the news (5) .... (finish). (6) .... (I / bring) you a cup?

VANESSA: No, don't bother. (7) .... (I / try) and go straight to sleep. Thanks anyway.

MICK: OK. Sleep well.

B Sandy and Alison are students who have been sharing a flat. Sandy is leaving to do a course abroad.

SANDY: It's hard saying goodbye after so long.

ALISON: Yeah. Remember to send me your address when (8) .... (you / get) to the States.

ANDY: Of course. (9) .... (I / probably / not / have) time next week because (10) .... (my course / start) the day after (11) .... (I / arrive), and (12) .... (I / spend) the weekend with some friends of my father's.

ALISON: Well, you can phone.

ANDY: Yes, OK. Do you know what (13) .... (you / do) this time next Sunday?

ALISON: (14) .... (I / get) ready to go to London.

ANDY: OK. So, (15) .... (I / phone) about three o'clock next Sunday.

ALISON: Great.

65 Choose the correct alternative.

1 Why did you walk all the way from the station? You ~~could phone~~ / <u>could have phoned</u> for a lift.

2 I loved staying with my grandparents when I was a child. They let me read all the books in the house and told me I <u>could go / was able to go</u> to bed as late as I wanted.

3 This carpet was priced at £500, but I <u>could get / was able to get</u> a discount because of this little mark in the corner.

4 I <u>couldn't have found / haven't been able to find</u> my diary for days. It's terribly inconvenient.

5 I've no idea where my brother is living now. He <u>can be / could be</u> at the North Pole for all I know.

6 It's difficult to understand how explorers survive the conditions they encounter in the Antarctic. I'm sure I <u>can't / couldn't</u>.

7 I wish I'd had your opportunities. With a proper education I <u>can be / could have been</u> a rich man now.

8 The day started off misty, but the sun had appeared by the time we reached the mountain and we <u>could climb / were able to climb</u> it quite quickly.

9 Our holiday flat had a kitchen. We <u>could cook / could have cooked</u> our own meals, but we preferred to go to local restaurants.

10 Why did I listen to you? I <u>can be / could have been</u> at home now instead of sitting here in the cold!

66 Complete the sentences with **could(n't)** and **was(n't) able to**. Sometimes there is more than one answer.

1 Eddie broke his leg last summer, so he ......*couldn't*...... swim.

2 Emily's handbag was stolen when she was out yesterday afternoon. Luckily she met a friend, so she .... use his mobile to call home.

3 I didn't enjoy the play because I forgot my glasses. I .... see the stage properly.

4 Marion's meeting was cancelled at the last moment, so she .... come to the sports club with us after all.

5 Robert .... speak any Dutch when he moved to Amsterdam last year, but he's almost fluent now.

6 I thought I'd have to get a taxi home from the party, but luckily I .... have a lift with Kate.

7 We really wanted to buy a house last year, but we just .... afford it.

8 My brother .... read well by the age of seven, but he's always had problems with maths.

9 Last night we heard a noise outside our window. When we turned off the light, we .... see a deer in the garden.

10 One day last week I locked my husband out of the house by mistake, but luckily he .... get in through an open window.

May and might

67 Answer the questions with **might** and the words in brackets.

1 Why is John wearing sunglasses? It's not sunny.
   (have some problem with his eyes)   *He might have some problem with his eyes.*

2 Why didn't Jane come to the party with her boyfriend last night?
   (have a row)   *They might have had a row.*

3 Why is Alan in such a bad mood today?
   (sleep badly last night) ....

4 Why is Anna looking under the desk?
   (drop something) ....

5 I can't remember where I put my bag.
   (be under the bed) ....

6 Why hasn't anybody said 'Happy Birthday' to me?
   (plan a surprise) ....

7 Why does Henry look so miserable?
   (have some bad news) ....

8 Why isn't Sophie in the office today?
   (work at home) ....

9 Why didn't Rosemary come to the cinema last night?
   (feel tired) ....

68 Use **might** to complete the sentences which explain why you should follow this advice.

1 You should reserve a seat on the train when you travel on public holidays.
   If you don't, *you might have to stand up for the whole journey* .

2 You'd better not carry that heavy suitcase.
   If you do, *you might injure your back* .

3 You should carry a map when you visit London.
   If you don't, ...

4 You should check the timetable before you leave for the station.
   If you don't, ...

5 You ought not to eat too many cream cakes.
   If you do, ...

6 You'd better have an early night.
   If you don't, ...

7 You should have your car serviced regularly.
   If you don't, ...

8 You shouldn't go to a party the night before your exam.
   If you do, ...

9 You ought to arrive punctually for work.
   If you don't, ...

10 You should eat plenty of fresh fruit and vegetables.
   If you don't, ...

Can, could, may, might, must and can't

69 Match the beginning of each sentence with the most suitable ending.

1 You must have met some fascinating people	*a* after all your hard work.	1	...d...
2 You must know Tokyo is expensive	*b* after touring the world for years.	2	....
3 You can't have lived in Tunisia for ten years	*c* if you've lived there.	3	....
4 You can't be tired	*d* during your trip to Africa.	4	....
5 You must be exhausted	*e* when you've just had a holiday.	5	....
6 You may find it difficult to settle down	*f* without learning some Arabic.	6	....
7 You couldn't have gone on holiday	*g* to the airport tomorrow.	7	....
8 You might think about going to Spain	*h* because you had a broken leg.	8	....
9 You could take a taxi	*i* for your next holiday.	9	....

70 Complete the email with the words from the box.

may be seeing	may not have done	could have fallen
~~may have left~~	couldn't have left	may be visiting
could be coming	may have found	

From: Robin Nicholas
To: Helena Shakespeare
Subject: Seeing you again

Helena

It was good to see you last week and to get your email yesterday.

Sorry to hear you lost your rap CD on the journey home. I've looked for it, but it definitely isn't in our car. I think you (1) *may have left* it on the train. Why not phone the lost property office?
It (2) .... down the side of your seat. Someone
(3) .... it and handed it in. Of course, if they like rap music,
they (4) .... ! Anyway, as far as I remember, you
(5) .... it here, because you were listening to it on the way to
the station.

And now my news. Guess what? I (6) .... to your part of the
world next month! There is a conference in your town which my boss wanted to attend, but now he's
heard that some important clients (7) .... our office at that time.

So, we (8) .... each other sooner than we expected. Let's
hope so. Of course it's not settled yet. I'll email as soon as I know for certain.

See you,
Robin

71 Choose the correct alternative.

1 You <u>must be</u> / <s>can't be</s> very proud of your son winning so many prizes.

2 We thought our cousins would visit us when they were in town last week, but they didn't even phone. I suppose they <u>must be</u> / <u>must have been</u> too busy.

3 The film's been such a big success. I guess it <u>must be</u> / <u>can't be</u> easy to get tickets to see it.

4 I'm sure you could mend this if you really tried. You <u>must be using</u> / <u>can't be using</u> the right tools.

5 I've just rung the garage to check whether they've fixed my car, but I can't get an answer. I suppose they <u>may have</u> / <u>may be having</u> a tea-break out in the yard.

6 I don't know why you wanted to stay at that party. You <u>might have enjoyed</u> / <u>can't have enjoyed</u> talking to all those boring people.

7 I can't go out this morning. We're getting a new sofa and the store <u>may be delivering</u> / <u>must be delivering</u> it today.

8 Please check these figures again. They're not accurate. You <u>might have been concentrating</u> / <u>can't have been concentrating</u> when you added them up.

9 You <u>must be</u> / <u>must have been</u> thirsty after carrying those heavy boxes. Shall I make some tea?

72 Complete the answers with **must**, **can't** or **might** and any other words you need.

1 GERALD: Can that be James phoning at this hour? It's gone midnight!
  HILDA: It ....*might be*.... him. He said he'd phone if he passed his exam.

2 JIM: There's a light on in that office block. Do you think it's a thief?
  HARRY: It ....*must be*.... the cleaners. They always work at night.

3 WILL: What are we having for Sunday dinner?
  TESSA: It .... chicken. Mum often does chicken on Sundays.

4 CLARE: Is that your daughter's coat?
  FIONA: No, it .... hers. It's much too big.

5 ANDY: Where did I put my trainers? I can't remember.
  JANE: They .... the car. You often leave them there.

6 ELINOR: Where did Adam get that new guitar? He hasn't got any money.
  KATE: It .... a present. After all, it was his birthday last week.

7 NICKY: Why did Mina ignore me at the party last night?
  RYAN: She .... you. She wasn't wearing her glasses.

8 EMMA: Do you think Cindy told the boss I left work early yesterday?
  NEIL: She's away this week, so she .... him.

9 JILL: What's making me feel so ill?
  PAT: It .... ate. Did you have seafood last night? That sometimes makes people ill.

Must(n't), need(n't), should(n't) and don't have to

73 Match the beginning of each sentence with the most suitable ending.

1 Lucy should be having breakfast,	*a* when she was supposed to be studying.	1 .....c.....
2 Patsy shouldn't go clubbing all night	*b* because she woke up early anyway.	2 ....
3 Jenny shouldn't have gone out	*c* ~~but she's too nervous to eat.~~	3 ....
4 Megan mustn't oversleep	*d* when she has an exam the next day.	4 ....
5 Nicky doesn't have to get up yet	*e* if she's not going to work today.	5 ....
6 Natalie didn't need to hurry	*f* or she'll be late for her interview.	6 ....
7 Sharon needn't have set the alarm clock	*g* because she wasn't late.	7 ....

74 Choose the correct alternative.

Thursday

NEIL: I'm doing a training session after work next Monday. Can you email these people?

ROBBIE: (1) <u>Must I do</u> / ~~Should I do~~ it now?

NEIL: Well, we (2) <u>must have sent / should have sent</u> them earlier really.

ROBBIE: Oh, all right then.

Friday

NAOMI: I've had an email about a training day on Monday. Do you think I (3) <u>must / ought to</u> take my laptop?

ELLIE: Well, you (4) <u>mustn't / don't have to</u>. But I always take mine, just in case I need it.

Monday

NAOMI: Hi, Neil. I've brought my laptop.

NEIL: Oh, you (5) <u>needn't bother / needn't have bothered</u>. There are plenty of computers. But why isn't Ellie with you? Is she away?

NAOMI: She wasn't asked to come. She's gone home.

NEIL: Oh, dear. The email (6) <u>must go / must have gone</u> to the wrong address. And I don't know where Robbie is. He (7) <u>must be / should be</u> here.

NAOMI: Well, he had to go out earlier. He (8) <u>must have missed / should have missed</u> the bus back. I expect he'll be here soon.

75 Complete the sentences with **must(n't)**, **needn't** or **should(n't)**.

1 We've run out of soap. I .....must..... get some more in the morning.
2 You .... finish that report tonight if you're too tired. Midday tomorrow is the deadline.
3 What are you doing here? .... you be at college?
4 He really .... have told his brother about this present. It was supposed to be a secret.
5 You .... bring your mobile because I've got mine with me.
6 You .... make so much noise. We'll be asked to leave if you don't stop it.
7 I'm going to be in trouble. I .... have emailed my brother yesterday afternoon and I completely forgot.
8 You .... have written a letter – a text message would have been OK.

76 Complete the second sentence with **must(n't)**, **need(n't)**, **should(n't)** or **(don't) have to** so that it has a similar meaning to the first sentence.

1 It is vital to wear a helmet when you ride a motorbike.
You ....must wear a helmet when you ride a motorbike................... .

2 I expect we'll get the contract because we offered the best price.
We offered the best price, so we ....

3 It isn't necessary for us to spend a long time in the museum if it's not interesting.
We ....

4 It was wrong of you to speak to my mother like that.
You ....

5 She promised to phone me before lunch. It's seven o'clock now.
She .... by now.

6 I made far more sandwiches than we needed.
I .... so many sandwiches.

7 It's essential that my father doesn't find out what I've done.
My father ....

8 In my opinion it would be wrong for them to move house now.
I don't think they ....

9 My sister offered me a lift, so it wasn't necessary for me to call a taxi.
As my sister offered me a lift, I ....

10 I think it's a good idea to check the timetable before we leave.
We ....

77 Read the rules of the Fitness Centre. Complete what the instructor says with **must(n't)**, **need(n't)** or **should(n't)**.

SPORTS CLUB NOTICE

- It is vital to have a health check before using the gym for the first time.
- It isn't necessary for members to pay for towels, but guests are charged £1 per towel.
- It is recommended that you begin with light exercises to warm up.
- It is not recommended that you exercise after a heavy meal.
- It's a good idea to ask a member of staff if you're not sure how to use the equipment.
- It is forbidden to use the Fitness Centre against the advice of the staff.

You (1) ......must..... have a health check before using the gym for the first time.
You (2) .... pay for towels, but your guests
(3) .... pay £1.
You (4) .... begin with light exercises to warm up.
You (5) .... exercise after a heavy meal.
You (6) .... ask a member of staff if you're not sure how to use the equipment.
You (7) .... use the Fitness Centre against the advice of the staff.

78 Read what James did. Then complete what the instructor says with **must(n't)**, **need(n't)** or **should(n't)**.

James became a member of the Sports Club yesterday. He used the gym without having a health check. He paid for a towel. He didn't begin with light exercises. He exercised soon after eating a big lunch. He didn't ask a member of staff how to use the equipment. His back is very painful today.

James (1) .... have used the gym without having a health check, so it's not my fault his back is very painful.
He (2) .... have paid for a towel.
He (3) .... have begun with light exercises.
He (4) .... have exercised soon after lunch.
He (5) .... have asked me how to use the equipment.
He (6) .... have injured his back.

(Don't) have to, should(n't), had better (not) and ought (not) to

79 Read the situations and write sentences with ought (not) to. Some of the sentences are past and some are present.

1 Andrew is very upset. You shouted at him.
  You ...ought not to have shouted at him.. .

2 Beatrice is in hospital. Her son hasn't been to see her.
  He ....

3 I live in Edinburgh. You went there last week, but you didn't visit me.
  You ....

4 Christopher has a new CD player. The children used it without his permission.
  They ....

5 The apple trees have lots of ripe fruit on them, but no-one can be bothered to pick it.
  Someone ....

6 Darren is five years old. He's playing with a box of matches.
  He ....

7 You've bought a new kitchen gadget. You thought the manufacturers provided an instruction leaflet, but you can't find it.
  There ....

8 We called at our friend's house, but she was out. We hadn't phoned her before we left home.
  We ....

80 Complete the sentences with **had better** where possible and **should** in the others.

1 You ...should.... always lock the front door when you go out.
2 I .... leave now, or I'll miss my bus.
3 I don't think people .... keep pets if they don't have time to care for them properly.
4 If you want to take photos while we're going round the museum, you .... ask permission. We don't want to get into trouble.
5 You .... wear a coat. It's cold outside.
6 Can you buy me some stamps when you go out? There .... be some change in my purse if you haven't got enough money.
7 I realise you must be surprised to find us here. Perhaps I .... explain what's going on.
8 People really .... wear a helmet when they ride a bike.
9 Passengers on long flights .... move their legs as much as possible.
10 Tell Jess that she .... get some money from the cash machine if we're going out tonight.

81 Complete the email with **had better, should** or **have to**. Sometimes there is more than one answer.

```
┌──────────────────────────────────────────────────────────────┐
│ □                                                        回 ▤ │
├──────────────────────────────────────────────────────────────┤
│   From:  Anna James                                          │
│     To:  Gary Newlands                                     ▲  │
│ Subject: Travel tips                                       ▼  │
├──────────────────────────────────────────────────────────────┤
```

Gary, I know you haven't travelled in this part of the world before so I (1) ....'d better.... give you a few tips to save you time and trouble.

First, you (2) .... make sure you get to the airport really early because you always (3) .... queue for ages at check-in. Then you (4) .... go through passport control and so on.

You (5) .... take something good to read because you'll have quite a long wait in the departure lounge. At least you (6) .... be able to sit down there. When your flight's called, you (7) .... follow an official out to your plane. You (8) .... (not) take very heavy hand luggage because you (9) .... carry it yourself and there aren't any trolleys. Everyone agrees there (10) .... be some, of course, but there aren't. The flight is quite short. You get a meal, which you (11) .... eat even if it doesn't taste very interesting, because you have a long bus journey at the other end. A colleague will meet you off the bus.

If you have any questions, email me and I'll get back to you as soon as I can. Anna

82 Complete the second sentence with **(don't) have to, should (not)** or **had better (not)** so that it has a similar meaning to the first.

1 It is compulsory to wear a helmet when you ride a motorbike.
You ...have to wear a helmet when you ride a motorbike... .

2 It's advisable to check that all the windows are shut whenever you go out.
You ....

3 It's not acceptable to borrow money from people you hardly know.
You ....

4 I suggest we keep the door shut in case someone sees us.
We ....

5 Training regularly is essential if you want to succeed in athletics.
You ....

6 I don't think it's a good idea to wear that bracelet in the street. It might get stolen.
You ....

7 Be sure to pick those tomatoes before they get too ripe.
You ....

8 There is no extra charge for delivery.
You ....

83 Tick (✓) the correct sentences.

1 *a* After a match, the captain insists the football team should take things easy. ✓
   b After a match, the captain insists the football team take things easy. ✓
   c After a match, the captain insists the football team to take things easy.

2 *a* The journalist demanded that the minister resigned.
   b The journalist demanded that the minister resign.
   c The journalist demanded that the minister should resign.

3 *a* If you really want to get rich fast, I suggest you should work harder.
   b If you really want to get rich fast, I suggest you work harder.
   c If you really want to get rich fast, I suggest you to work harder.

4 *a* He never has any money, so it's very odd that he have a new car.
   b He never has any money, so it's very odd that he has a new car.
   c He never has any money, so it's very odd that he should have a new car.

5 *a* I think the weather will stay dry, but you can borrow my raincoat if by any chance it rains.
   b I think the weather will stay dry, but you can borrow my raincoat if by any chance it should rain.
   c I think the weather will stay dry, but you can borrow my raincoat if by any chance it rained.

6 *a* My doctor explained that it was important I should take more exercise.
   b My doctor explained that it was important I take more exercise.
   c My doctor explained that it was important I took more exercise.

84 There are mistakes in five of these sentences. Correct the sentences where necessary.
Write 'OK' if the sentence is already correct.

1 We were very surprised that Tom behave in such a rude manner.   *that Tom behaved*

2 I asked a shop assistant for directions and he recommended to try the tourist information office.

3 The police accepted the recommendation that they reduce the number of officers on duty.

4 If I can't leave my bags here, what do you suggest me to do with them?

5 I shouldn't go in there if I were you. They're having an argument about money.

6 Should be I out when you call, just leave a message with my assistant.

7 It's essential that I should see the doctor today.

8 Why didn't you demand Colin to pay you the money?

50

85   Complete the conversation with **should** where necessary. Leave out **should** where possible.

BEN: I can't find the sales reports anywhere. What (1) ..*should I do*.. (I / do)?

SUE: I really don't know. It's typical that (2) .... (they / disappear)
       just when you need them. Why don't you ask Rose?

BEN: I did. She insisted that (3) .... (I / search) for them.

SUE: She's so unhelpful.

BEN: And where's Jack? He promised to check them with me.

SUE: I saw him in the coffee bar a few minutes ago.

BEN: It's essential (4) .... (he / see) the reports.

SUE: Shall I send someone to fetch him?

BEN: No, (5) .... (I / not / bother). He'll probably turn up in a
       minute.

SUE: OK. Are you going to stay in the office over lunchtime?

BEN: Yes. It's important (6) .... (I / find) these reports. We'll be
       using them in this afternoon's meeting.

SUE: Oh, right, yes. Well, I'm going to look at some computers. And look,
       (7) .... (anyone / call), will you say I'm not available till
       tomorrow? I really haven't got any spare time today.

BEN: Are we going to get a new computer?

SUE: Well, the manager's recommendation is that (8) .... (we / wait)
       until later in the year.

BEN: Why's that?

SUE: He says prices may fall. He suggests (9) .... (we / wait)
       until the autumn.

BEN: I suppose it's only natural (10) .... (he / be) cautious.

SUE: Hmm.

86 Use your own ideas to complete the sentences.

1 In most countries motorcyclists must ...*wear a helmet*.. .
2 I nearly overslept this morning. I should have ....
3 The plane lost one engine, but luckily the pilot was able to ....
4 The traffic is very bad this afternoon, so I may ....
5 Politicians ought not to ....
6 I don't really like this job, so I might ....
7 Lots of my friends have passed that exam, so it can't be ....
8 I don't know why my brother hasn't arrived. He may have ....
9 If you really want to get fit, you should ....
10 We were so short of money we had to ....
11 I don't know why you didn't get my letter. It must have ....
12 The car broke down, but luckily we were able to ....
13 I could .... when I was ten, but I couldn't ....
14 It's getting very late. You'd better ....

87 Read this notice. Then complete the advice for people who are coming to your school or place of work.

Information for newcomers to London Language Institute

- You shouldn't leave your car unlocked.
- You should buy a notebook.
- You mustn't be late for class.
- You must attend classes every day.
- You needn't bring a dictionary.
- You don't have to take any exams.

Information for newcomers to ....

1 You shouldn't ....
....
2 You should ....
....
3 You mustn't ....
....
4 You must ....
....
5 You needn't ....
....
6 You don't have to ....
....

88 Choose the correct alternative.

1 If <u>I miss</u> / ~~I'll miss~~ the bus this afternoon, I'll get a taxi instead.
2 We'll have to go without John if <u>he doesn't arrive / he won't arrive</u> soon.
3 They <u>won't refund / didn't refund</u> your money if you haven't kept your receipt.
4 Will you send me a postcard when <u>you reach / you'll reach</u> Mexico?
5 If I make some coffee, <u>do you cut / will you cut</u> the cake?
6 <u>Did you work / Would you work</u> harder if you were better paid?
7 If you <u>don't complain / didn't complain</u> so much, you might be more popular.
8 <u>Weren't my friends / Wouldn't my friends be</u> envious if they could only see me now!

89 Complete the questions.

1 EVA: I don't know what's happened to my dictionary. I've looked everywhere for it.
  SUE: What ….._will you do_…. if you don't find it?
  EVA: I suppose I'll have to buy a new one.

2 TIM: I'm thinking of applying for the manager's job.
  ANN: Really? How ……………………………………………… if you got it?
  TIM: Oh, about £2,000 a year more than now, I suppose.

3 MAY: I don't know what I'm going to do about money. I haven't even got enough for my rent this week.
  LEE: ……………………………………………… if I lent you some?
  MAY: Well, it would help, of course. But I can't borrow from you.
  LEE: Don't be silly. How much do you want?

4 JESS: I hope the weather's OK when I'm on holiday next week.
  STEVE: What ……………………………………………… if it rains?
  JESS: I've no idea. I've never been to Malta before.

5 PAUL: I wish I could afford a new car.
  TINA: What ……………………………………………… if you could afford one?
  PAUL: Oh, I wouldn't mind what make it was, as long as it didn't keep breaking down.

6 BILL: I don't think I'm going to pass my driving test next week.
  BEN: What ……………………………………………… if you don't?
  BILL: I won't be able to get the job I want. They said I must be able to drive.

90   Put the verbs into the correct form.

1 If I had more money, ...~~would you marry~~.... (you / marry) me?

2 He wouldn't help you if .... (he / not / like) you.

3 .... (you / find) the machine is quite simple to operate if you
look at the manual.

4 .... (your parents / not / be) proud if they could see you now?

5 If .... (I / not / revise) thoroughly, I may fail my test.

6 If you wanted to buy someone a really good present, what sort of thing
.... (you / look for)?

7 Sally would have a lot more friends if .... (she / not / be)
so mean.

8 How .... (you / feel) if you were in my situation?

9 Would you change your job if .... (you / can)?

91   Lisa is talking to her friend Trish about what she might do when she leaves university.
Write sentences using the words given.

TRISH: Do you have any plans for next year?

LISA: Well, I don't have any money. But (1) I / travel / if I /afford it.
........~~I'd travel if I could afford it.~~..

TRISH: (2) If you / find / a job abroad / you / take it?
....

LISA: (3) If it / be / somewhere I want to go / I / certainly / consider it
carefully.
....

TRISH: What about working as an 'au pair', looking after children
in a family?

LISA: (4) I / only / consider / that if I / be / sure about the family.
....

....

(5) If they / not / treat / me well, I / be very miserable.
....

TRISH: Yes. (6) You / have to / be / sure to use a good agency.
....

There's a website I've seen.
(7) I / find / you the address of it if you / be interested.
....

LISA: Yes, I am. (8) If I / decide / to apply to an agency, / you / help me write a letter?
....

TRISH: Of course. Well, I hope you succeed, whatever you decide to do.

LISA: Thanks very much. I'll let you know.

TRISH: That's OK.

92 Write questions using **if** for the following answers.

1 <u>What would you do if someone gave you a</u>
   <u>diamond necklace</u> ?

I'd probably give it to my mother.

2 _____ ?

I'd share it with my friends.

3 _____ ?

I'd call the police.

4 _____ ?

We'd get out as fast as we could.

5 _____ ?

I'd ask my teacher's advice about it.

6 _____ ?

He'd be extremely angry.

7 _____ ?

She'd probably fall over.

8 _____ ?

I'd be late for work.

9 _____ ?

We'd sail around the world.

10 _____ ?

They'd never make any money.

11 _____ ?

There'd be no more wars.

12 _____ ?

I'd stay at home all day.

93 Look at the questions you wrote for Exercise 92. Now write new answers of your own to your questions.

1 What would you do if someone gave you a diamond necklace?
   <u>I'd sell it and buy a horse.</u>

2 _____

3 _____

4 _____

5 _____

6 _____

7 _____

8 _____

9 _____

10 _____

11 _____

12 _____

If I did and If I had done

94 Match the beginning of each sentence with the most suitable ending.

1 If you had been promoted,	a you'd be able to change the system.	1 ....e....
2 If you were rude to the boss,	b would you have left the firm?	2 ....
3 If you were promoted,	c you wouldn't be sacked.	3 ....
4 If you hadn't been promoted,	d you wouldn't get a reference.	4 ....
5 If you had lost your job,	e would you have made any changes?	5 ....
6 If you apologised,	f you'd probably regret it later.	6 ....
7 If you were fired,	g you'd have been very upset.	7 ....

95 Complete the conversations.

1 SEAN: Why didn't you go to the party last night?
  JIM: I wasn't invited.
  SEAN: So _would you have gone_ if you _'d been invited_ ?

2 JILL: Jane's got a university degree, hasn't she?
  MILLY: Yeah. I don't know how she can work here. I .... a job
         doing something exciting if I .... her qualifications.
  JILL: What kind of job would you want?
  MILLY: Oh, I don't know exactly. But if I .... Jane, I
         .... to meet interesting people and visit interesting places.

3 SAM: Why did you ask Veronica about her boyfriend? It really upset her.
  MICK: Well, I didn't realise they'd split up.
  SAM: You didn't know, then?
  MICK: Of course not. If I .... , I ....
        her about him.

4 TIM: Hey, look at that motorbike. What a beauty!
  PAT: Look out! Mind that litter bin.
  TIM: Ouch! I've hurt my leg.
  PAT: Well, you .... it if you ....
       where you were going.

5 JOHN: Do you love me?
  ROSE: You know I do.
  JOHN: Would you .... if I .... poor?
  ROSE: Probably. But fortunately you're rich.
  JOHN: Well, yes, I am. But if I .... all my money, what
        .... ?
  ROSE: I'd say goodbye.
  JOHN: Now you're joking.
  ROSE: Oh no, I'm not!

96 Read the letter. For each number, write a comment beginning with **if**.

> Dear Ryan,
>
> It was great to hear from you. Thanks for the congratulations and good wishes. I'll pass them on to Charlie when I see him at the weekend. Of course we're very excited about getting married, and frantically busy too, needless to say. You ask how we met.
>
> Well, it's quite a funny story. **(1)** Do you remember I failed one of my final exams? That meant I had to spend part of the summer in college. And that meant I couldn't go on holiday with my family. **(2)** The travel company refused to give me a refund because I cancelled too late. I was really fed up about not going on holiday with Mum and Dad. Then something nice happened. **(3)** I think the travel agent felt sorry for me because he had failed his final exams when he was a student. **(4)** Anyway, he had a cancellation on a tour which started later in the summer. So he was able to offer to transfer my booking. I was really pleased. **(5)** My father was pleased too, as transferring the booking meant that his money wasn't being wasted. So, I went on this tour. And I met this young man. He was on his own too. **(6)** He told me his girlfriend should have been with him, but they'd had a row and she'd refused to come. **(7)** We were the only ones travelling alone, so we found ourselves going round the sights together. **(8)** He hadn't read about the places we were visiting and I spent most of my time telling him about them. And that was it really. We found we'd fallen in love. **(9)** Wasn't it lucky I failed that exam? That's how I met my future husband!
>
> Now I must rush off and do some shopping. Will you come and stay soon? It'd be lovely if you could meet Charlie. Write soon. What have you been up to recently?
>
> Lots of love,
>
> Cherry

1   If she hadn't failed one of her final exams, she wouldn't have had to spend part of the summer in college.

2   ....

3   ....

4   ....

5   ....

6   ....

7   ....

8   ....

9   ....

97   What would you say in each situation? Begin each sentence with If.

1   *yesterday*   *today*

If I hadn't dyed my hair, my friends wouldn't be laughing at me.

2   *yesterday*   *today*

If I hadn't revised thoroughly, I wouldn't be able to do the test.

3   *yesterday*   *today*

4   *this morning*   *now*

I haven't got time for breakfast.

I can't concentrate.

5   *last week*   *now*

I must remember to phone and book seats.

BOOK NOW FOR CONCERT

BOOK NOW FOR CONC SOLD OUT

6   *8 am*   *9.30 am*

Oh damn!

You're fired!

7   *last weekend*   *today*

I'm sorry I won't be at the wedding.

8   *this afternoon*   *now*

Do we need to stop for petrol?

No, we've got more than enough to get home.

98   Use your own ideas to complete the sentences.

1 What will you do if <u>you miss your plane</u> ?
2 He'd have more friends if he ....
3 If I hadn't mended the TV, we ....
4 You wouldn't have felt ill if you ....
5 If she didn't gossip about her friends, she ....
6 Will you forgive me if I .... ?
7 What would happen if I .... ?
8 If he had listened to my advice, he ....
9 She would have won the competition if she ....
10 They wouldn't have minded if we ....

99   Complete the sentence for each situation. Study the examples carefully.

1 You should take more exercise because that's the way to get fit.
If you <u>take more exercise</u> , you <u>'ll get</u> fit.

2 Road travel is cheaper than rail travel in this country. As a result we have lots of traffic jams.
If road travel <u>weren't (wasn't) cheaper</u> than rail travel in this country, we <u>wouldn't have</u> lots of traffic jams.

3 Cutting down rainforests has caused many plants and animals to disappear.
Many plants and animals <u>wouldn't have disappeared</u> if people <u>hadn't cut down</u> rainforests.

4 I can't take much exercise because I don't have enough free time.
If I .... more free time, I ....

5 Many people leave their cars unlocked when they park. This makes life easy for thieves.
If people .... , life ....

6 Some people didn't realise that smoking was dangerous when they were young. Now they are middle-aged they have serious health problems.
If people .... , they .... now they are middle-aged.

7 Peter sowed some seeds, but they didn't grow because he forgot to water them.
The seeds .... if Peter ....

8 It's important to protect wildlife now. Otherwise there will be nothing left for future generations.
If we .... , there .... for future generations.

9 People don't realise the importance of energy conservation, so they do nothing about it.
If people .... , they .... something about it.

100 Look at the pictures and write what each person wishes, using the words given.

1

be / tall and strong
...... I wish I were tall and strong. ......
or ...... I wish I was tall and strong. ......

2

have / car
....

3

work / office
....

4

live / with my son
....

5

Help!

can / swim
....

6

not / live / city
....

7

be / helicopter pilot
....

8

not / have / short hair
....

101 Bernie and Martin share a room at college. Read what they say about each other. Then write sentences beginning **I wish he would / wouldn't**.

MARTIN

It's dreadful having to share a room with Bernie. He's so untidy! His books are all over the place, he never washes his coffee cup, he leaves dirty clothes around the room – it's such a mess I can't work. And he comes in late in the evening when I'm trying to sleep and lies in bed watching television. I can't stand it! I'm going to look for a room on my own.

The trouble with Martin is that he never relaxes. He works so hard. He gets angry, but he won't tell me what's wrong. And he interferes with my possessions. He moves my books around so I can't find them. It's not much fun sharing a room with Martin.

BERNIE

Martin says:
I wish Bernie wouldn't leave his books all over the place.
....
....
....
....

Bernie says:
I wish Martin would relax sometimes.
....
....
....
....
....

102   Complete the conversations using wish.

1   SUE: My mother's really angry with me.
    PAM: Why?
    SUE: Because she found out I left my job.
    PAM: Oh, yes. I told her that.
    SUE: Well, I ....._wish you hadn't told_.... (not / tell) her. It's not your business.
    PAM: I'm sorry.

2   TONY: Have you seen Ben's new jacket? I bet it was expensive.
    ANA: He told me it cost him £500.
    TONY: I .... (have) as much money as him.
    ANA: Well, you may not be rich, but you're much better-looking than Ben.
    TONY: Am I?

3   GARY: You seem to enjoy dancing with Lionel.
    JANE: Yes, I do. He's a very good dancer.
    GARY: I .... (learn) to dance when I was young.
    JANE: You could learn now.
    GARY: Oh, I'd feel stupid in a dancing class at my age.

4   EVA: I went to Norway last month.
    MAY: Really? My brother's living in Oslo now.
    EVA: I .... (know). I could have visited him.
    MAY: Yes, it's a pity. You must tell me if you're going there again.

5   FRED: My parents moved to New York last month.
    ANDREW: How do they like it?
    FRED: My mother likes it, but my father misses their old home.
              He .... (not / move) there.
    ANDREW: Perhaps he'll get used to it.
    FRED: I doubt it.

6   JANICE: You haven't seen my car keys, have you?
    WENDY: No I haven't.
    JANICE: I .... (know) what I'd done with them.
    WENDY: I hope you didn't leave them in the car door.
    JANICE: So do I!

7   KAY: My brothers are digging a swimming pool.
    JILL: That sounds like hard work!
    KAY: It is. Actually, I suspect they .... (never / start).
              But they can't stop now. There's a great big hole in the middle of the garden.
    JILL: Yes, I see what you mean.

03 Complete the sentences using words from each box.

| build   design   direct   discover   discover   invent   ~~name~~   paint   play   write |

| the Ancient Egyptians   Crick and Watson   Marie Curie   Gustave Eiffel
~~Eric the Red~~   Angelina Jolie   Akira Kurosawa   Guglielmo Marconi
Picasso   Philip Pullman |

1 Greenland *was named by Eric the Red* .
2 *Northern Lights* ....
3 The Pyramids ....
4 The wireless ....
5 *Guernica* ....
6 Lara Croft ....
7 The Statue of Liberty ....
8 The structure of DNA ....
9 *The Seven Samurai* ....
10 Radium ....

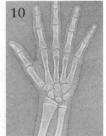

104 Put the verbs into the correct present perfect form, active or passive (**has done** or **has been done**).

1

the woman / open
....The woman has opened it....

the tree / cut down
....The tree has been cut down....

3

the puncture / mend
....

4

the dishes / wash
....

5

Jane Jones / elect
....

6

the rabbit / disappear
....

7

the sculpture / steal
....

8

the students / pass
....

05 Rewrite the newspaper article using passive forms of the underlined verbs.

DARING RAID AT LOCAL HOTEL

Thieves (1) <u>held</u> the manager of the Ridgeway Hotel at gunpoint last night during a daring raid in which they (2) <u>took</u> nearly £50,000 from the hotel safe. They also (3) <u>broke</u> into several of the bedrooms and (4) <u>removed</u> articles of value.

The thieves made their escape through the kitchen, where they (5) <u>damaged</u> several pieces of equipment. They (6) <u>injured</u> the chef when he tried to stop them and (7) <u>left</u> him lying unconscious on the floor. Police (8) <u>arrested</u> the thieves early this morning.

The manager of the Ridgeway Hotel says, 'I'm very relieved the thieves have been caught!'

1 The manager of the Ridgeway Hotel was held at gunpoint last night.
2 ....
3 ....
4 ....
5 ....
6 ....
7 ....
8 ....

06 Put the verbs into the correct passive form.

1 I've collected all the documents that .....*are needed*..... (need) for the house sale. Can you take them to the lawyer's office .....*to be signed*..... (sign)?

2 Look, this is a secret. Come into the garden where we .... (not / overhear).

3 If you hadn't been so late for work, you .... (not / sack).

4 This office is very inefficient. The phone .... (never / answer) promptly, no proper records .... (keep), and, worst of all, no reports .... (written) since I started work here.

5 I was so worried about my garden while I was in hospital, but I have very good neighbours. When I got home, I could see that the vegetables .... (water) every day and the grass .... (cut) regularly.

6 Can you come to the police station? The man who .... (suspect) of stealing your wallet .... (arrest) and .... (question) at the moment. The police hope he .... (identify), either by you or another witness.

7 We had hoped to see several famous paintings, but the gallery .... (reorganised) at the time of our visit and most of the really valuable works .... (move) for safe keeping.

107 There are mistakes in eight of these sentences. Correct the sentences where necessary. Write 'OK' if the sentence is already correct.

1 My neighbour is proud of her grandson <u>who born last week.</u>   _who was born last week_

2 I'm very fond of this old brooch because it <u>was belonged</u> to my grandmother   ....

3 My family live in Scotland, but I was educated in France.   ....

4 I'm afraid I can't lend you my camera. It's repairing this week.   ....

5 The bridge was collapsed during the floods, but fortunately no-one was using it at the time.   ....

6 If you aren't careful what you're doing with that hammer, someone will hurt in a minute!   ....

7 The word 'stupid' was in my report, but it wasn't referred to you.   ....

8 I'm sorry I'm late. I got held up in the traffic.   ....

9 When did you discover that the money had been disappeared?   ....

10 Children under the age of seven do not allow in this pool.   ....

108 Choose the correct alternative.

Dear Sally,

How are you? I've been having a great time here in England. I'm being looked after very well by our cousins. I (1) <s>was taken</s> / <u>have been taken</u> sightseeing twice since I arrived and I (2) <u>have been introduced /</u> have introduced to some of their friends, who (3) <u>have made / were made</u> me feel very welcome.

Last night I (4) <u>have shown / was shown</u> around a castle by the owner! Most of the land in this area (5) has <u>been owned / has owned</u> by his family for about five hundred years. Apparently the land (6) <u>was given /</u> has been given to them after one of his ancestors (7) <u>was killed / has killed</u> while trying to save the king's life. Quite romantic, isn't it?

The castle itself was a bit disappointing, to be absolutely honest. The owner told us that it (8) <u>was suffered /</u> suffered serious damage during a fire about thirty years ago. When it (9) <u>was restored / restored</u>, they (10) <u>were added / added</u> central heating and things like that. So once you're inside, it (11) <u>doesn't feel / isn't felt</u> much different to any other large, old house.

But the owner is a real character. He told us lots of stories about when he was young. He (12) <u>was sent /</u> sent abroad to work in a bank, but he (13) <u>hated / was hated</u> it. So he (14) <u>has behaved / behaved</u> very badly in order to (15) <u>get sacked / got sacked</u>. He kept us laughing for hours. I hope he (16) <u>was invited / will be invited</u> to our cousins' house before I leave so that I can hear some more stories.

I'll have lots more to tell you when I get back.

Love,

Maurice

109 Complete the second sentence so that it has a similar meaning to the first sentence.
Do not use **by** unless it is important to the meaning.

1 The teacher has marked all the homework.
All the homework _has been marked_ .

2 My boyfriend kept me waiting for half an hour.
I _____ .

3 The students must pay all their own fees for this course.
All the fees for this course _____ .

4 Do you suppose your brother could have written that email?
Do you suppose that email _____ ?

5 They use a computer to do that job nowadays.
A computer _____ .

6 During the summer, the café was employing more waiters every week.
During the summer, more waiters _____ .

7 Nobody informed the police that there had been a mistake.
The police _____ .

8 Where will your company send you next year?
Where will you _____ ?

9 The news about the war worried Josephine.
Josephine _____ .

10 I've still got the camera because no-one has claimed it.
I've still got the camera because it _____ .

11 Has anyone ever asked you for your opinion?
Have you _____ ?

12 The children shouldn't have opened that parcel.
That parcel _____ .

13 All visitors must wear identity badges.
Identity badges _____ .

14 Someone must have changed the time of the meeting.
The time of the meeting _____ .

15 Is anyone using this computer?
Is this computer _____ ?

110 Put the verbs into the most suitable passive tense.

Alana has just met her boyfriend Grant at a café.

ALANA: Hi! Sorry I'm late.

GRANT: What kept you?

ALANA: I came on the bus and it (1) ....was stuck.... (stick) in a traffic jam for forty minutes.

GRANT: Why didn't you just walk across the park as usual?

ALANA: Because the park

(2) .... (close) since last weekend.

GRANT: Why's that?

ALANA: A film (3) .... (shoot) there.

GRANT: Do you know who it

(4) .... (direct) by?

ALANA: No, but I think Leonardo DiCaprio is in it. Someone told me he

(5) .... (see) at the Royal Hotel at the weekend.

GRANT: Really?

ALANA: Yeah. He (6) .... (fly) here in a private plane by the film company.

GRANT: Well, if it's true, we're not going to the disco at the Royal this Friday.

ALANA: Why not?

GRANT: If he's there, the hotel (7) .... (surround) by fans and security guards.

ALANA: But we might meet him if we go.

GRANT: Don't be silly. He won't be at the disco. And we certainly

(8) .... (not invite) to his room.

ALANA: I suppose not. But we can go to the park gate now and see what's happening. Perhaps we (9) .... (ask) to act in a crowd scene. I heard that some local people (10) .... (employ) as extras yesterday, but I was too busy to go.

GRANT: OK, if you want to. But I don't think we

(11) ....

(allow) anywhere near the filming.

111 Complete the sentences with the correct form of **get** where possible and a form of **be** in the others.

1 I never found that book we were looking for. It .....got..... lost when we moved house.

2 After the way he behaved last time he went to their house, it's unlikely he .... asked there again.

3 Naturally this vase is expensive. After all, it .... believed to be over three hundred years old.

4 I phoned to explain what had happened, but I .... cut off before I could finish.

5 There isn't any cheese left, I'm afraid. It .... eaten by the children.

6 He is a well-known expert on animal diseases and his opinions .... greatly respected.

7 My sister will be thrilled if her design .... chosen.

8 The book .... torn when the children started fighting over who should read it first.

9 Please don't touch anything on my desk. You .... supposed to answer the telephone, not tidy the office.

10 She was quite friendly at first, then she .... promoted and now she doesn't care about us any more.

112 Complete the second sentence so that it has a similar meaning to the first sentence.

1 It is said that house prices are too high.
House prices ....are said to be too high... .

2 It is thought that the hospital is short of money.
The hospital ....

3 It was alleged that the athlete had cheated.
The athlete ....

4 It is reported that the prime minister is resigning.
The prime minister ....

5 It is expected that the new sports stadium will be finished soon.
The new sports stadium ....

6 It is generally considered that sixteen is too young to get married.
Sixteen ....

7 It was thought that the book had been destroyed.
The book ....

8 It is believed that the children had been hiding for two weeks.
The children ....

113 Look at these notes made by a journalist. Then complete the article he wrote for a magazine. Use verbs in the correct passive form.

Kitchen
6 am visit market, choose vegetables and fruit
7 am plan menu
8 am unload meat
9 am cook staff breakfast
9.30 am make desserts
10 am wash vegetables
    clean fish
    put meat in oven
    mix salads

Dining-room
11 am vacuum floor
    lay tables
    arrange flowers
12 open doors
    serve about 200 meals every lunchtime

I t's exactly midday and I'm sitting in the Beverly Restaurant. Today I've been finding out just how much work goes on in a restaurant before the first customers arrive. The staff have already done six hours work. The day began with a visit to the market where vegetables and fruit (1) .....were chosen..... . Back at the restaurant the menu (2) .... and then the day's delivery of meat (3) .... After that, breakfast (4) .... for the staff. But they didn't have long to eat it, because by 9.30 it was time for the desserts (5) ....
After the vegetables (6) .... , the fish (7) .... and the meat (8) .... in the oven. While this was happening in the kitchen, in the dining-room the floor (9) .... Since then, the tables (10) .... and the flowers (11) .... , so the dining-room looks fresh and pretty. In the last few minutes, salads (12) .... in the kitchen and in a moment the doors (13) .... In the next three hours, about two hundred meals (14) .... !

114 Tanya wants to rent a flat, but it needs some work before she can move in.
She talks to the landlord and he agrees to her suggestions.
Complete the conversation using **have** + the verbs in brackets.

TANYA: This flat is in a good place, but there are a few problems.

LANDLORD: Oh, really? What do you mean?

TANYA: The mirror is broken.

LANDLORD: (1) _I'll have it replaced._ (replace)

TANYA: There are marks on the carpet.

LANDLORD: (2) .... (clean)

TANYA: I don't like the colour of the walls.

LANDLORD: (3) .... (paint)

TANYA: All the furniture is in the wrong rooms.

LANDLORD: (4) .... (rearrange)

TANYA: One of the chairs is broken.

LANDLORD: (5) .... (mend)

TANYA: Several of the cupboards are full of old clothes.

LANDLORD: (6) .... (empty)

TANYA: The curtains are dirty.

LANDLORD: (7) .... (wash)

TANYA: Then I might rent the flat.

115 Rewrite the <u>underlined</u> words using **have something done**.

1 I didn't recognise Sheila because <u>the hairdresser's dyed her hair</u>.
   she's had her hair dyed

2 I've been getting a lot of annoying phone calls, so <u>the telephone company is going to change my number</u>.
   ....

3 Gabrielle broke her leg six weeks ago, but she's much better now. In fact <u>the doctors should be taking the plaster off tomorrow</u>.
   ....

4 Rowland has made a lot of money, so <u>an architect's designed him a fine new house</u>.
   ....

5 This room gets hot when the sun shines, so <u>I'm employing someone to fit blinds on the windows</u>.
   ....

6 I heard that Mrs Green didn't trust her husband, so <u>she hired a detective to follow him</u>!
   ....

7 My sister had always been self-conscious about her nose, so she decided to go to a clinic <u>for an operation which will straighten it</u>.
   ....

116 Wilma Shriek the pop singer has just arrived in London from America. She's being interviewed by a journalist. Look at the journalist's notes and Wilma's answers. Then write the journalist's questions.

1 how long / be here? — How long are you going to be here ? — Two months.
2 be / first visit to this country? — Is this your first visit ? — No, it isn't.
3 when / be here before? — ? — Five years ago.
4 why / come then? — ? — For a holiday.
5 why / come this time? — ? — To work.
6 do / a tour now? — ? — Yeah, that's right.
7 how many cities / visit? — ? — About twenty.
8 what / want to do after that? — ? — Have a holiday.
9 have / message for your fans? — ? — Yeah – come to our concerts and have a wild time.

117 Lucy works in a tourist information office and has to answer a lot of questions. Read her answers and complete the questions using the words in brackets.

1 TOURIST: Do you know where the city maps are ? (city maps)
  LUCY: Over there, on the other counter.

2 TOURIST: Can you tell me .... ? (this guidebook)
  LUCY: £5.99.

3 TOURIST: I'd like to know .... (postcards)
  LUCY: They're on the third shelf, beside the window.

4 TOURIST: Do you happen to know .... ? (the last bus)
  LUCY: Yes, it leaves at half past ten on weekdays and ten at weekends.

5 TOURIST: Could you explain .... ? (this timetable)
  LUCY: It's quite simple. You find your destination on the left and read the times across the page.

6 TOURIST: Please could you tell me .... ? (the museum)
  LUCY: It's in the High Street, next to the library.

7 TOURIST: Do you know .... ? (the music festival)
  LUCY: The last weekend of July.

8 TOURIST: I can't remember .... (the castle)
  LUCY: It was built about 1450, so that makes it over five hundred years old.

118 Sonia Schmidt is phoning to book a hotel room. Complete the conversation by putting the words in the correct order. Do not change the form of the words.

RECEPTIONIST: Good morning. Falcon Lodge Hotel.

SONIA: Hello. My name's Schmidt. I'd like to book a room please.

RECEPTIONIST: Certainly. (1) staying / how many nights / you / be / will

   How many nights will you be staying ?

SONIA: Three. Starting next Thursday.

RECEPTIONIST: Yes, we have rooms available. Double or single?

SONIA: Double please. (2) available / is / one with a sea view

   .... ?

RECEPTIONIST: Yes. By the way, (3) have / the special offer / about / are running / we / you / at the moment / heard

   .... ?

SONIA: No.

RECEPTIONIST: It's four nights for the price of three. (4) don't / take advantage / you / it / why / of

   .... ?

SONIA: (5) have / for it / what / I / to do / to qualify / got

   .... ?

RECEPTIONIST: Just confirm your reservation in writing and pay a ten per cent deposit.

SONIA: (6) be / much / would / that / how

   .... ?

RECEPTIONIST: £21.

SONIA: Yes. I think I'll do that. We can stay till Monday. (7) to / make / the cheque / who / I / should / payable

   .... ?

RECEPTIONIST: Falcon Lodge Hotel.

SONIA: OK. I'll post it today.

RECEPTIONIST: Thank you very much. We'll look forward to seeing you.

SONIA: Thank you. Goodbye.

RECEPTIONIST: Thank you.

119 Brian has decided to join a Health Club. First, the instructor helps him to plan his fitness programme. Write the instructor's questions. Read the whole conversation before you begin.

INSTRUCTOR: OK, Brian. Let's find out how fit you are.
(1) First of all, _how old are you_ ?

BRIAN: I'm thirty-two.

INSTRUCTOR: (2) And .... ?

BRIAN: About seventy-five kilos.

INSTRUCTOR: (3) And

.... ?

BRIAN: One metre eighty.

INSTRUCTOR: (4) .... ?

BRIAN: I'm a bus driver.

INSTRUCTOR: Really? (5) So, ... ?

BRIAN: Well, I take some exercise, but it's not regular.

INSTRUCTOR: (6) .... ?

BRIAN: No, I haven't done any sport since I left school. I just work in the garden and sometimes go for a walk on my day off.

INSTRUCTOR: I see. (7) .... ?

BRIAN: Yes, I admit I do. Not more than a packet a day, though.

INSTRUCTOR: That's quite a lot, actually.
(8) .... ?

BRIAN: I tried once, about a year ago, but I got so impatient I nearly crashed my bus.

INSTRUCTOR: Well, perhaps we can give you some help. It's really important, you know. Now if you'll come with me, I'm going to do a few checks and then we'll make a plan for you.

BRIAN: OK. Thanks.

120 There are mistakes in eight of these sentences. Correct the sentences where necessary. Write 'OK' if the sentence is already correct.

1 Have ever you been to Thailand? — _Have you ever been_
2 What is this word mean?
3 How much costs it to fly to Australia from here?
4 We can't remember where did we put our passports.
5 Had the play already started when you got to the theatre?
6 Now, come and sit down. Would you like to explain what is the problem?
7 How long did it you take to get here?
8 Now I understand why didn't you tell me about your job!
9 Excuse me. Can you tell me where the dictionaries are?
10 Why young people don't show more respect to the elderly?

74

121 Read the email. Then write what Angela actually said to Della.

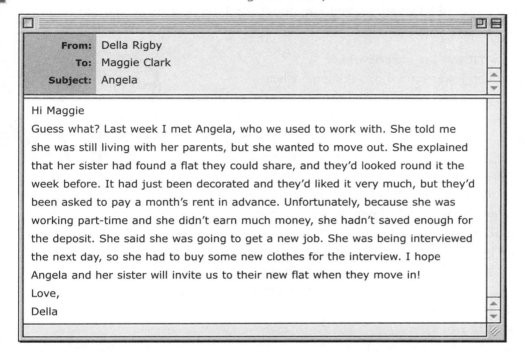

From:	Della Rigby
To:	Maggie Clark
Subject:	Angela

Hi Maggie

Guess what? Last week I met Angela, who we used to work with. She told me she was still living with her parents, but she wanted to move out. She explained that her sister had found a flat they could share, and they'd looked round it the week before. It had just been decorated and they'd liked it very much, but they'd been asked to pay a month's rent in advance. Unfortunately, because she was working part-time and she didn't earn much money, she hadn't saved enough for the deposit. She said she was going to get a new job. She was being interviewed the next day, so she had to buy some new clothes for the interview. I hope Angela and her sister will invite us to their new flat when they move in!

Love,

Della

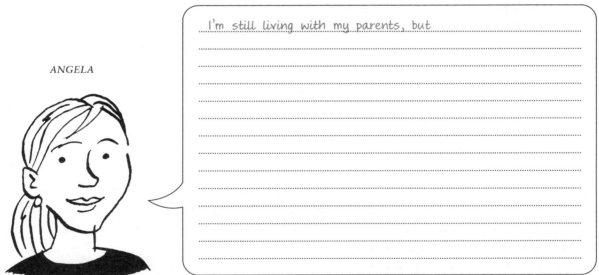

ANGELA

I'm still living with my parents, but

122

In Exercise 41, Alex, who wanted to go to an art college, was interviewed by one of the lecturers. A year later, his friend Charlie asked him about the interview, as he wanted to go to the same college. Complete Alex's answers.

CHARLIE: So, Alex, what was the interview like?

ALEX: Well, the interviewer started by asking me when I (1) ...'d left... (leave) school. And then he wanted to know where I (2) .... (be) since then. I told him I (3) .... (have) several jobs. First I (4) .... (work) in a café for about a year because I (5) .... (need) to save a lot of money for travelling. Of course he asked me where I (6) .... (want) to go and when I told him, he asked whether I (7) .... (visit) all those places. I explained to him that I (8) .... (be) to Brazil and Peru, and I (9) .... (spend) some months in Turkey. He told me I (10) .... (be) very lucky. Then he asked if I (11) .... (bring) some work to show him and he looked at my work. He liked it, I think.

CHARLIE: Was that all?

ALEX: I think so. He asked me when I (12) .... (become) interested in painting and drawing, and I said that I (13) .... (think) I always (14) .... (be). Oh, yes, and he told me my work (15) .... (be) very good.

CHARLIE: I'm not surprised. It is good. I hope he'll like my stuff too.

ALEX: Oh, I think he will, actually.

123

Look back at your answers to exercise 116. Complete the article which the journalist wrote a month after the interview with Wilma.

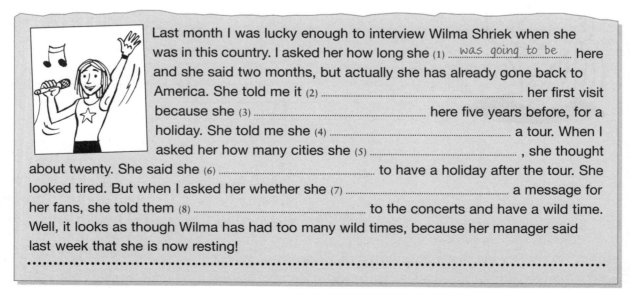

Last month I was lucky enough to interview Wilma Shriek when she was in this country. I asked her how long she (1) ...was going to be... here and she said two months, but actually she has already gone back to America. She told me it (2) .... her first visit because she (3) .... here five years before, for a holiday. She told me she (4) .... a tour. When I asked her how many cities she (5) ...., she thought about twenty. She said she (6) .... to have a holiday after the tour. She looked tired. But when I asked her whether she (7) .... a message for her fans, she told them (8) .... to the concerts and have a wild time. Well, it looks as though Wilma has had too many wild times, because her manager said last week that she is now resting!

124 John had a row with his girlfriend, Julie. His friend Mark tried to help them get back together and talked to Julie for John.

MARK: Julie, John's asked me to talk to you.

JULIE: I don't want to speak to him.

MARK: Look Julie, John's really upset.

JULIE: I'm upset too.

MARK: Will you just let me tell you his side of the story?

JULIE: I'm not interested. He promised to meet me at the restaurant, but he didn't turn up. I don't want to see him again.

MARK: But Julie, his car had broken down.

JULIE: So? I had my mobile with me.

MARK: But that's the point. He tried to phone, but he couldn't get through.

JULIE: I don't believe he tried.

MARK: Yes, he did. His mobile wasn't working, so he came to my flat and tried on my phone. Do you believe me?

JULIE: OK, I'll talk to him. Listen, I'm going to be late for work. I'll meet him at six o'clock in the square.

MARK: Thanks, Julie. He'll be really happy. And I promise he'll be there.

Complete the conversation Mark had later with John.

JOHN: What did Julie say?

MARK: She said she (1) ___didn't want to speak to you___ .

JOHN: Well, what did she say when you told her I was really upset?

MARK: She said she (2) .... too, so I asked her to let me tell her your side of the story. She said she (3) ....
You (4) .... to meet her at the restaurant, but you (5) .... She said she (6) .... again.

JOHN: Did you explain about the car?

MARK: Yes, and she said she (7) .... her mobile with her. So I explained you couldn't get through, but she said she (8) .... you (9) ....
Then I told her you (10) .... to my flat and (11) .... on my phone. I asked her (12) .... me. I think she did. Anyway, she said she (13) .... to you. Then she said she (14) .... late for work, so we had to finish. You have to meet her in the square at six o'clock.

JOHN: Thanks, Mark. I really appreciate what you've done for me.

MARK: That's all right. Just don't be late this evening.

125 You've just arrived at a hotel for a holiday. It's not the same as your travel agent told you it would be. Look at the pictures in your travel agent's brochure and complete the fax you send to your travel agent.

IMPERIAL HOTEL

They serve an NO international menu in the dining-room.

The gardens have a wonderful variety of flowers. NO

There's a large NO swimming pool.

A disco is held every night. NO

You'll love the NO private beach.

A fitness centre has been added to the hotel's facilities. NO

You can go NO horse-riding.

Room service is NO available.

The tennis courts can be booked free of charge. NO

Guests can use the nearby golf course free of charge. NO

FAX

TO: Mr Smiley, Sunways Travel Agency

I am very disappointed because the Imperial hotel is quite different from what you told us. You said there ......*was a large swimming pool*...... and that a disco

You also said ....

The brochure said ....

You told us ....

....

In fact, none of these facilities is available. Please arrange for us to be transferred to a better hotel immediately.
Yours,

....

126 Anna has just met the singer Colin Boyle. (You may remember him from Exercise 16.) She is telling Ian, about the meeting. Ian wants to know exactly what Colin said to Anna and what she said to him.

IAN: Well, what was he like? Was he friendly? What did he say?

ANNA: He was really friendly. (1) He asked me who I was.

IAN: Then what?

ANNA: (2) He asked me where I came from.

IAN: And what did you say?

ANNA: (3) I told him I came from Dublin, of course. Then (4) he said that was where he was born too. Then (5) I told him I'd been a fan of his for ages and (6) he said that was very good to hear. Then (7) he asked whether I was going to the concert tonight. So (8) I told him we wanted to, but we hadn't been able to get tickets. (9) He asked if the tickets were sold out, and (10) I told him they'd sold all but the most expensive ones and we couldn't afford those.

IAN: And did he give you some tickets?

ANNA: No, he didn't. But (11) he asked the concert hall manager if we could have some at the cheaper price. And the manager said 'Yes'!

Now write exactly what Anna and Colin said.

 1 Colin asked: .....Who are you?...

 2 Colin asked: ....

 3 Anna said: ....

 4 Colin said: ....

 5 Anna said: ....

 6 Colin said: ....

 7 Colin asked: ....

 8 Anna said: ....

 9 Colin asked: ....

10 Anna said: ....

11 Colin asked the concert hall manager: ....

127 Imagine that when you were on holiday last year you met someone famous. This could be a musician, a film star, a politician, etc. Look at what Anna told Ian and write an email to a friend about your conversation.

From:	....
To:	....
Subject:	....

Hi!

I never told you that when I was on holiday last year I met ....

....

....

128 Rewrite the sentences beginning in the way shown.

1 'Where are you going?' asked Tom.
   Tom asked (me) where I was going .

2 'Where are you going to spend the holiday?' asked Mike.
   Mike asked ....

3 'What will you do when you leave school?' asked Jennifer.
   Jennifer asked ....

4 'How did you know my name?' the nurse asked the doctor.
   The nurse wanted to know ....

5 'Do you have an appointment?' asked the clerk.
   The clerk asked ....

6 'Have you seen my car keys?' Bernard asked his wife.
   Bernard wondered ....

7 'Why didn't Isobel phone me?' asked her brother.
   Isobel's brother wanted to know ....

8 'Will you carry my briefcase for me please, Rosemary?' Richard asked.
   Richard asked ....

9 'When can I see the doctor?' Charles asked the receptionist.
   Charles asked ....

129 Complete the sentences with the correct form of **say** or **tell**.

1 _Did you tell_ (you) your brother the truth about that money?
2 What .... (you) to Wendy last night? She looks terribly upset this morning.
3 Is something wrong? Can you .... me about it?
4 My little sister kept asking me .... her a story, but I couldn't think of one.
5 If I asked you to marry me, what .... (you)?
6 I never know what .... to people when they pay me a compliment.
7 Don't worry, I'm sure the boys are fine. Anyway, I .... them to call me if they had any problems.
8 I'll never speak to him again after all the lies he .... me last weekend.
9 If I were you, I .... (not) anything to the police about your suspicions until you have more evidence.
10 Promise you .... (not) anything to my parents. They'll be furious if they find out what I've done.
11 I .... (already) you, I don't know where your diary is.
12 Please .... you'll forgive me. I'm really sorry for all the trouble I've caused.
13 I'm ready to serve the meal. Can you .... the children to go and wash their hands, please?

130 Complete the email with the correct form of **say** or **tell**.

From: Neville Cripps
To: Stephanie Peters
Subject: Discussion with my father

Dear Stephanie,

I'm writing (1) ..._to tell_.. you about the discussion I had with my father last weekend. We talked for several hours and I (2) .... him all about the plans we've made for our business. At first, he wasn't very interested, he (3) .... he didn't think we were old enough to run a business. However, I (4) .... him that we had already seen the bank manager, who (5) .... that the plan seemed realistic. So then he sat down and asked me (6) .... him how much money we'd need to start with, and where we'd sell the stuff we made, and so on. Eventually he (7) .... to me, 'OK, it's a good plan. (8) .... Stephanie that I'll lend you some money to get started.' Honestly, I couldn't believe he (9) .... it! Isn't it great? I'm really looking forward to seeing you next week so we can talk to him together and get things going.

All the best,

Neville

131 There are mistakes in four of these sentences. Correct the sentences where necessary. Write 'OK' if the sentence is already correct.

1 Joan said she had been very happy in her new job and liked her new boss better than her old one.

Joan said she was very happy

2 Michael explained that he couldn't come to the party because he was working that evening.

....

3 We had a great evening with Janet. She was saying us about her fascinating trip to Kenya.

....

4 I'm sorry to bother you, but you said to call if I was worried.

....

5 We were disappointed when the receptionist told that the hotel was fully booked that week.

....

6 The museum guard asked the visitors to not touch the exhibits.

....

7 The tour guide explained that the Severn is the longest river in England.

....

132 Put the verbs into the correct form: –ing or infinitive.

1. I don't get on with the new boss, so I've asked ___to be transferred___ (transfer) to another branch of the company.

2. Please stop ___interrupting___ (interrupt) me when I'm explaining something to you. You can ask questions at the end.

3. He admits .... (enter) the house, but he says he didn't take anything.

4. What a dreadful man! Can you imagine .... (live) with him?

5. I've forgotten .... (bring) my briefcase with me. I'll have to go back for it.

6. We had hoped .... (live) in our new house by now, but the builders are still working on it.

7. I don't mind .... (work) late if it will help at all.

8. You'll just have to find a job. I simply can't afford .... (support) you any longer.

133   Put the verbs into the correct form: **–ing** or infinitive.

CYCLIST ABANDONS 24 HR RIDE

For the second time, Andrew Spicer, the local cycling star, has decided (1) ...._to give up_.... (give up) the attempt (2) .... (ride) his bike non-stop for twenty-four hours. His decision came after poor weather conditions had caused him to postpone (3) .... (set off) for several hours. His first attempt had also ended in failure, when he appeared (4) .... (lose) control of his bicycle as he attempted to avoid (5) .... (hit) a small child and crashed into a wall. He says that he has not yet decided whether (6) .... (try) one more time, but denies (7) .... (lose) interest in the project. 'I've promised (8) .... (raise) money for the local hospital,' he explained. 'They deserve help. I shall do what I can if I manage (9) .... (find) the time.'

134   Complete the conversations with suitable verbs in the correct form: **–ing** or infinitive.

A   ANN: What are you doing this weekend?

    BILL: I'm hoping (1) ...._to visit_.... my parents if I can.

    ANN: I thought you went to see them last weekend.

    BILL: No, I planned (2) .... them, but they suggested (3) .... the visit for a week because they hadn't finished (4) .... the spare room.

B   CILLA: Can you help me with these packages?

    DAVE: Of course.

    CILLA: I've got to get them all posted today. One of our main customers has said he'll consider (5) .... to another supplier if we don't improve our delivery times.

    DAVE: Have we been failing (6) .... on time? I didn't know that.

    CILLA: Apparently someone forgot (7) .... one order last month. So I agreed (8) .... them myself this time – we can't risk (9) .... such an important customer.

C   JACK: Oh dear, here's another email from Peter.

    SEAN: Why does he keep (10) .... you?

    JACK: He wants me to join his basketball team. He's offered (11) .... me repair my car if I agree (12) .... them. The trouble is, I'd have to go to a lot of practice sessions and I haven't got time. And I can fix the car by myself.

    SEAN: Well, you'll just have to find a way to say no. You can't avoid (13) .... to him for ever.

135 Complete the sentences using **–ing** or infinitive.

1 *Can you help me?*
TERRY   CHRIS

Terry wanted Chris ....to help him..... .

2 *Sit!*
ANGELA   JASON

Angela ordered ....

....

3 CASHIER

The gangsters forced ....

....

4 LAURA   DELLA

I wish I'd never bought those drums.

Laura regretted ....

....

5 FELICITY

You're not going out till you've finished your homework.

CHARLIE

Felicity made ....

....

6 SOAP   SHAMPOO   CONDITIONER

JOHN

John tried ....

....

7

The car needed ....

....

8 SANDRA

JIM

Jim helped ....

....

136 Complete the conversations with the correct form of the verbs and any other words you need.

A PAT: Who should I ask if I want a day off?

MICK: It doesn't really matter, except I'd advise (1) ....*you not to ask*.... (not / ask) the assistant manager. He can be very rude sometimes.

PAT: Oh, I don't mind (2) .... (shout) at by him. He threatened (3) .... (sack) me last week, but he apologised very politely later.

B SUE: I don't trust the manager's new secretary.

JILL: Why not?

SUE: Well, she claims (4) .... (work) in several other banks before she came here. But when I asked her about them, she kept (5) .... (change) the subject. I was wondering whether (6) .... (say) something to the manager.

JILL: Perhaps she's just shy. Why don't we go on (7) .... (be) friendly for a few more days and see how she behaves?

SUE: OK. I'd hate (8) .... (get) someone into trouble for nothing.

C ANDY: I don't know what to do about Gemma. She's so difficult to work with. She keeps forgetting (9) .... (pass) on important messages and she won't let me (10) .... (help) her when she's busy.

JOAN: Have you actually talked to her about all this?

ANDY: That's part of the problem. I've tried (11) .... (discuss) the problem with her, but she always says she's too busy to stop and talk. I've even tried (12) .... (ask) her to have lunch with me, but she doesn't want to.

JOAN: I think I'd better have a chat with her. How long has she been like this?

ANDY: Oh, it's several weeks now.

JOAN: Well, I'd really like (13) .... (know) about the problem earlier. Never mind, I'll see what I can do.

ANDY: Thanks very much.

137 Complete the sentences with your own ideas. Use –ing or the infinitive.

1 I often help ...*to prepare lunch at weekends*.................................... .

2 I learnt .... at the age of ....

3 I can't help .... when I see someone being treated unfairly.

4 I don't mind .... , but I hate ....

5 I sometimes pretend .... when really I'm just daydreaming.

6 I always encourage .... which I have enjoyed reading myself.

7 I remember .... when I was a small child.

8 I enjoy .... even though I'm not very good at it.

9 I expect .... by the end of next year.

10 I've given up ....

138 Match the beginning of each sentence with the most suitable ending.

How to study efficiently

1 Begin by	*a* making plans you can't possibly keep.	1 ....b....
2 Be realistic: there's no point in	*b* making a list of what you have to do.	2 ....
3 Find a quiet place where you can work without	*c* studying.	3 ....
4 If possible, use this place only for	*d* marking each topic on your list as you complete it.	4 ....
5 Check you have everything you need before	*e* jumping up to fetch things every five minutes.	5 ....
6 This means you won't waste time	*f* being interrupted.	6 ....
7 Encourage yourself by	*g* starting work.	7 ....

139 Use the notes to complete the advice below. Use **–ing** and a preposition if necessary.

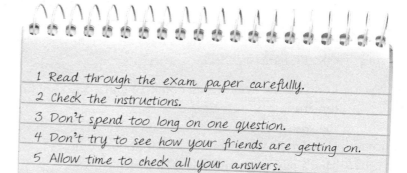

1 Read through the exam paper carefully.
2 Check the instructions.
3 Don't spend too long on one question.
4 Don't try to see how your friends are getting on.
5 Allow time to check all your answers.
6 Cheats rarely do well in the long run.

How to take exams

1 Begin _by reading through the exam paper carefully_ .
2 Make sure you know exactly what to do ....
3 There's no point ....
4 Don't waste time ....
5 Avoid careless mistakes ....
6 It's rarely worth ....

140 Complete the pieces of advice. Use **–ing** and your own ideas.

1 You should take regular exercise instead of _sitting in front of the television all day_ .
2 You can't earn a lot of money by ....
3 It's rude to borrow people's things without ....
4 You must always thank people for ....
5 You mustn't insist on ....
6 It's wrong to make accusations without ....
7 It's good manners to apologise for ....
8 You should fill up with petrol before ....

141 Put the verbs into the correct form.

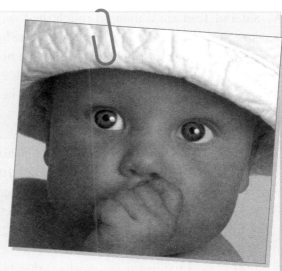

Dear Ruth,

Thanks very much for the lovely present you sent for Laurie.

It was very kind of you. You say in your note that you haven't got used to (1) ....being.... (be) an aunt yet. I used to (2) ....think.... (think) that becoming a father wouldn't change me. I was wrong, of course! Life will never be the same again. We never used to (3) .... (go) to bed before midnight, but now we're asleep by ten because we've had to get used to (4) .... (wake) up at five o'clock. Actually, in a way, that's good. I always used to (5) .... (arrive) late at the office, but since Laurie was born my colleagues have got used to (6) .... (find) me hard at work by the time they arrive!

I should say, though, it hasn't been so easy for Jenny. At first she found it very hard on her own with Laurie. She wasn't used to (7) .... (spend) all day alone with a baby. But now she's got to know a neighbour who also has a young baby and that helps. She used to (8) .... (say) she'd go back to work when Laurie was six months, but now she's used to (9) .... (be) at home she's beginning to enjoy herself, so she may wait until Laurie is a bit older.

Anyway, try to come and see us soon while Laurie is still small.

All the best,

Dennis

142   Complete the conversations. Use a preposition + **–ing** or the infinitive.

A   Sid and Tom are walking through the town centre.

SID: Look, there's Angela. Isn't she lovely?

TOM: She's all right. You really like her, don't you?

SID: Oh, yes. I often dream (1) _about taking_ (take) her out for a meal or a film, but I'm afraid (2) _to ask_ (ask) her.

TOM: Why?

SID: Well, I suppose I'm afraid (3) .... (look) foolish if she refuses.

TOM: If you like her so much, you shouldn't be afraid (4) .... (risk) it. Anyway, I'm sure she won't refuse.

SID: Really? OK, I'll phone her tonight.

TOM: Good. I'm glad I've succeeded (5) .... (persuade) you to phone her.

SID: Why do you say that?

TOM: I happen to know she rather fancies you. I told her I'd make you phone her! She'll be looking forward (6) .... (hear) from you!

B   Brian and Phil are at work.

BRIAN: Good morning Phil, could we have a word in my office?

PHIL: Of course.

BRIAN: I'm sorry (7) .... (have) to say this, but I'm afraid you failed (8) .... (achieve) high enough sales to earn a bonus this month. I suppose the bad weather kept the customers away?

PHIL: Yes, I guess so. I'm very sorry (9) .... (let) you down this time.

BRIAN: OK, I'm sure you'll make it up soon. I'm thinking (10) .... (send) one or two junior sales staff on a course next month. Would you be interested (11) .... (go)?

PHIL: Yes, I would be.

BRIAN: Good. I'll put your name on the list.

PHIL: Thank you.

C   Joanna has phoned Katie

JOANNA: I'm sorry (12) .... (forget) your birthday last week.

KATIE: That's OK. You were in the middle of your exams. You're allowed (13) .... (forget) people's birthdays on exam days!

JOANNA: That shouldn't have prevented me (14) .... (send) you a card. Did you get some from the family?

KATIE: Well, Mum was the only one (15) .... (remember).

JOANNA: Well, she's not likely (16) .... (forget), is she?

KATIE: No, I suppose you're right.

Verb forms: review

143   Put the verbs in the correct form. Can you solve this detective puzzle?

Trevor Stern was not a popular man, in spite of his wealth.
He (1) ....*lived*.... (live) in a large house about a mile outside the
village of Prenton. When he (2) ....*was found*.... (find) dead in
his study, no-one (3) ....*cried*.... (cry), not even his only daughter.
It was soon clear that he (4) .... (murder).

Detective Inspector Blackledge took
statements from his widow
Dorothy, his seventeen-year-old
daughter Lucy, his business partner
Gerald Brook, and his doctor.

DOROTHY

I (5) .... (not / love) my husband, he was a cold and selfish man. But I
(6) .... (not / murder) him, either. After dinner last night he said he
(7) .... (want) to check some business papers in his study. He
(8) .... (have) a meeting with Gerald, his business partner, the next
morning. He (9) .... (ask) for some tea. That was about nine o'clock. I
(10) .... (watch) a rather exciting film on television, so I
(11) .... (tell) Lucy to take it to him.
    At quarter past nine Doctor Emerson (12) .... (call). I
(13) .... (notice) the time because we (14) .... (expect)
him to come earlier. I (15) .... (answer) the front door bell. Trevor
(16) .... (shout) in his study. He and Lucy (17) ....
(obviously / have) a serious row. So I (18) .... (take) the doctor into the
sitting-room for a moment. Then Trevor stopped (19) .... (shout). I
guessed Lucy (20) .... (go) out by the back door. Doctor Emerson went to
the study. I think he wanted to persuade Trevor (21) .... (go) into hospital
for some tests, but Trevor (22) .... (not / want) to go.
    I (23) .... (hear) my husband shouting again several times over the next
twenty minutes. He called Emerson an ignorant country doctor and later he said something
like, 'There's nothing you can do!' I think Lucy (24) .... (come) back into
the house while the doctor (25) .... (still / talk) to Trevor.
I (26) .... (hear) the front door bang during a moment of quiet when
Trevor (27) .... (not / shout). I was tired and fed up, and went to my
bedroom soon after that. My sister (28) .... (phone) and
we (29) .... (talk) for ages. I (30) .... (tell) her
I (31) .... (decide) to leave Trevor.

Mum (32) .... (watch) a stupid film after dinner, so she made me
(33) .... (take) Dad's tea into his study. It was about nine o'clock. He was
in a really mean mood. He shouted at me because I (34) .... (spill) a few
drops of tea on his desk while I (35) .... (pour) it. I
(36) .... (not / want) to watch the film, so I (37) ....
(creep) out of the house by the back door. I (38) .... (decide) to go down
to the village and use the public phone to call Alan. He's my boyfriend.
I (39) .... (never / like) Mum or Dad to be around when I
(40) .... (talk) to him. Especially yesterday, because Dad and I
(41) .... (have) a stupid argument about Alan the day before.
   It (42) .... (usually / take) quarter of an hour to walk to the village.
Perhaps it (43) .... (take) less time last night. I can't prove I
(44) .... (go) to the village. No-one (45) .... (see) me
while I (46) .... (walk) there. I (47) .... (see) Gerald,
that's Dad's business partner. He (48) .... (stand) near the window in his
sitting-room. He (49) .... (not / see) me though, because it was dark
outside. He (50) .... (talk) on the phone, I think. Alan
(51) .... (not / answer) the phone. Then I (52) ....
(remember) he (53) .... (tell) me he (54) .... (play) in
a concert that evening. So I (55) .... (walk) home again. I
(56) .... (meet) Gerald just before I (57) .... (reach)
our house. He (58) .... (look) for his dog. That was about twenty to ten.
I came in by the back door as quietly as possible and went to bed. I didn't want to see my
parents again that evening.

LUCY

DOCTOR EMERSON

I (59) .... (call) at the Sterns' house at 9.15. I (60) ....
(be) rather later than I (61) .... (plan) to be because I
(62) .... (visit) another patient. When Mrs Stern (63) ....
(let) me into the house, she (64) .... (seem) rather embarrassed and
(65) .... (show) me into the sitting-room. I could hear Trevor Stern
(66) .... (shout) at someone in his study. Mrs Stern said something about
teenage girls and that they (67) .... (have) problems with Lucy. Well, the
shouting (68) .... (stop) almost immediately, so I (69) ....
(go) to his study. Lucy (70) .... (already / leave) the room before I
(71) .... (get) there. I tried (72) .... (explain) to
Trevor why he needed (73) .... (have) these hospital tests, but he
(74) .... (not / listen). He said I (75) .... (be) an ignorant
country doctor who (76) .... (not / know) what he (77) ....
(talk) about. I (78) .... (realise) it was no use (79) .... (argue)
with him, so I (80) .... (leave) after only a few minutes. I was quite angry
actually. I let myself out of the house without (81) .... (see) Lucy or Mrs Stern.

Yes, Trevor was my business partner. We (82) .... (not / be) really friends.
Yes, my house (83) .... (be) just round the corner from the Sterns'. I
(84) .... (live) here for two years now. I (85) ....
(have) a little cottage in the village. But I (86) .... (buy) this house when I
started (87) .... (earn) a lot of money.

   I can't really tell you very much about the night Trevor died. I took my dog for a long
walk that evening. I (88) .... (go) up on the hills, away from the village.
Then the stupid dog (89) .... (go) after a rabbit or something and I
(90) .... (lose) him in the dark. I (91) .... (look) for
him when I (92) .... (meet) Lucy, as a matter of fact. She
(93) .... (walk) up the road towards their house. She
(94) .... (seem) rather upset. I told her I (95) ....
(look) for my dog, but she said she (96) .... (not / see) it.

   She (97) .... (go) into her house and I (98) ....
(find) the dog a few minutes afterwards. I was back home by just after quarter to ten.

GERALD

Detective Inspector Blackledge showed the statements to her colleague, Sergeant Ross.

BLACKLEDGE: Well, Ross. What do you think? Who killed Stern?

ROSS: I don't know. It (99) .... (not / be) his wife. She
(100) .... (not / even / go) into the study.

BLACKLEDGE: But she admits she didn't love him. Do you think she's in love with the doctor?

ROSS: It's possible. And perhaps Trevor Stern (101) .... (find out).
But we know the doctor was at the hospital by ten o'clock that night.
And that's at least half an hour from the Sterns' house.

BLACKLEDGE: But that (102) .... (mean) he (103) ....
(leave) the Sterns' house before half past nine.

ROSS: Exactly. Also, Dorothy Stern told her sister she (104) .... (leave)
her husband. She didn't need (105) .... (murder) him.

BLACKLEDGE: Yes, and there's something about Lucy's story which doesn't quite fit.
Let's see, what did Gerald Brook say?

ROSS: That's it! Lucy (106) .... (not / walk) to the village and
back if he (107) .... (meet) her at twenty to ten.
She (108) .... (still / shout at) by her father at 9.15.

BLACKLEDGE: But look at all the statements. The times don't fit.

ROSS: Neither do the facts. Someone (109) .... (tell) lies.

BLACKLEDGE: I think it's time we (110) .... (make) an arrest.

Who did they arrest? See page 120.

Countable and uncountable

144 Some of these sentences need **a/an**. Correct the sentences where necessary.

1 Joanna eats apple every morning.   ....an apple................................
2 Peter doesn't like milk in his tea.   ....Ok..
3 Katie rarely has biscuit with her coffee.   ....
4 George normally eats meat for dinner.   ....
5 Brian usually has omelette for lunch.   ....
6 Margaret never drinks beer.   ....
7 Robin occasionally puts butter on his potatoes.   ....

145 Jane is trying to lose weight, so every day she writes down what she has eaten. Look at the picture of what she ate today and complete her diary entry, using **a/an** where necessary.

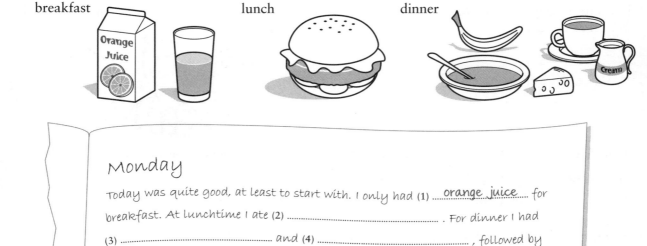

breakfast   lunch   dinner

Monday

Today was quite good, at least to start with. I only had (1) ......**orange juice**...... for breakfast. At lunchtime I ate (2) .... For dinner I had (3) .... and (4) .... , followed by (5) .... I had (6) .... afterwards and I'm afraid I put (7) .... in it!

146 Do you have a healthy diet? Doctors advise us to avoid eating too much fat and salt, and to eat at least five portions of fruit or vegetables every day. What did you eat yesterday? Look at Jane's diary entry. Write a similar diary entry for yourself.

DIARY   Date:

47 There are mistakes in seven of these sentences. Correct the sentences where necessary. Write 'OK' if the sentence is already correct.

1 To use this computer, you need a permission from the boss.   _you need permission_

2 We're looking for a place to rent.   _OK_

3 We're late because the traffics are terrible.   ....

4 He had to leave the college because of a bad behaviour.   ....

5 I phoned my brother to wish him good luck for his exam.   ....

6 It's a pity Rebecca had her hairs cut short.   ....

7 It's not a bad room, but the furnitures take up too much space.   ....

8 As an old friend, may I give you an advice?   ....

9 We didn't have the most up-to-date information.   ....

10 The check-up was less unpleasant experience than I had expected.   ....

48 Complete the conversation with the words from the box. Sometimes you need the plural (–s). Use some of the words more than once.

case   day   experience   luggage   paper   room   scenery   weather   view

Mary and Liz are about to go on holiday together. Mary has come to collect Liz in her car.

MARY: Hello, Liz, are you ready?

LIZ: Yes, just about. All my (1) ......_luggage_...... is here. I hope I haven't got too many (2) ......_cases_...... .

MARY: Don't worry. There's plenty of (3) .... in the car.

LIZ: Oh, good. I've packed rather a lot of things. I haven't had much
(4) .... of travelling in the mountains, so I wasn't sure what to bring.

MARY: As long as you've got some warm sweaters for the evenings, and a good raincoat, you should be OK. The (5) .... in the mountains is wonderful, but the
(6) .... can change very suddenly.

LIZ: Well, we've got a lovely (7) .... to start with.

MARY: You're right there. And I'm sure you'll like our (8) .... at the hotel, because they've promised me the ones I had last year when I was with my brother. Did you pack the guidebook, by the way?

LIZ: Yes, and I packed some (9) .... so we can do some drawing.

MARY: That's a good idea. It'd be nice to keep some sort of diary too.

LIZ: Yes. We might make an album afterwards, with words and pictures. And I'm sure I'm going to have some great (10) .... to write about.

MARY: Well, the (11) .... are like nothing you've ever seen. And there's always music or something in one of the villages every evening. We'll buy the local
(12) .... when we get there and find out what's going on.

LIZ: Well, I'm ready.

MARY: OK, let's go!

149 Complete the description with **a/an**, **some** or **the**.

HOLIDAY FLAT

In (1) ...._the_.... bedroom of this flat there are twin beds, (2) ...._a_.... cupboard, and (3) .... chair. There are (4) .... extra pillows on top of (5) .... cupboard. In one corner there is (6) .... basin.

   There is also (7) .... basin in (8) .... bathroom. (9) .... basin in (10) .... bathroom is bigger. Above it there is (11) .... shelf for towels.

This flat has (12) .... modern kitchen. In (13) .... middle of (14) .... room is (15) .... table which has (16) .... chairs around it.

Now write two more sentences of your own about the flat.

17 ....

18 ....

50 Write a description of your home in about 80 words.

....

....

....

....

....

....

51 Put in a/an or the.

Tina wants to buy a car. She has come to see Ryan, who is trying to sell his.

TINA: So, you don't say much in your advert. Is this (1) ...*an*.... old car?

RYAN: Not very old. Come and have a look at it.

TINA: Were you (2) .... first owner?

RYAN: No, I got it two years ago.

TINA: Have you driven it a lot?

RYAN: Well, I drive to my office in (3) .... city centre five days (4) .... week, but I don't use it much at weekends.

TINA: I see. Now, the thing is, I'm (5) .... doctor. I've just started work at (6) .... hospital in Hills Road. I'm on call a lot of the time and I have to find (7) .... car which is really reliable. (8) .... car I used to have was always breaking down and giving me problems.

RYAN: Oh, this one's very good. It may not be (9) .... fastest car around, but it always gets there eventually. And it's got (10) .... new set of tyres.

TINA: Right. It's good to know that. Can I go for (11) .... test drive?

RYAN: Um, actually, that's not possible right now.

TINA: Why not?

RYAN: Well, basically, I'm afraid it won't start. You see, (12) .... battery is flat.

152 Put in **the** where necessary. If **the** is not necessary, leave the space empty (–).

Portrait of a family: (1) .....The..... Walshes

There are three adults and four children in this family. (2) .....The..... children are Sandra, aged seventeen, Craig aged eleven, Michelle who is eight and (3) .....–..... little Ryan, who is nearly one. Their parents are Jack and Sylvia. (4) .... other adult is Irina, who is Sylvia's mother. They live near Liverpool, a large city in (5) .... north-west of England.

On (6) .... weekday mornings everyone gets up early. Jack Walsh works for a company which makes (7) .... glass. He leaves at seven o'clock. He likes to avoid (8) .... rush hour, he says. Sylvia suspects that really he likes to avoid having breakfast with (9) .... children, who are very noisy.

Craig and Michelle catch (10) .... school bus at eight-fifteen. Sandra is at (11) .... art school, studying photography. She lives away from (12) .... home during term-time, so she avoids (13) .... noise too.

Ryan doesn't go to (14) .... school yet, of course. Next year, he will start at (15) .... nursery school where (16) .... other children used to go. His grandmother looks after him while his mother is at (17) .... work. She works at (18) .... Tate Gallery which is beside (19) .... River Mersey in (20) .... centre of Liverpool.

153 Write a similar description of a family you know or a famous family.

....

....

....

....

....

....

154 In these news items **the** has sometimes been used in the wrong place. Read the items carefully and cross out **the** where it is not necessary.

The Prime Minister left this morning for a tour of the Far East. He will visit ~~the~~ Singapore and the Malaysia and then go on to the Philippines, where he will make a speech about the environment.

The King Juan Carlos of the Spain arrived in London today for a three-day visit to the United Kingdom. He was met by the Queen and drove with her to the Buckingham Palace. Tomorrow he will have the lunch with the Governor of the Bank of England and in the evening he will have talks with the businessmen.

A conference is taking place in the Mexico City on ways of helping the unemployed in the developing world. A report will be sent to the United Nations, but it is feared that the unemployment will remain a problem in the most countries for many years to come.

55 While you were on holiday, some thieves stole your wallet. You saw them, but they got away. Complete the description you gave to the police.

1 All *of them had fair hair* .
2 None *of them was older than forty* .
3 Both *(of) the men were wearing T-shirts* .
4 One *of the men had a shoulder bag* .
5 All .
6 None .
7 Both .
8 Both .
9 Both .
10 Neither .
11 Neither .
12 One .

56 Use the words in the first box to make true statements about the people in the second box.

(a) few (of)   all (of)   both (of)   lots (of)   most (of)   neither of   none of   one of   some (of)

bands   classmates   cousins   doctors   friends   grandfathers   neighbours   parents   politicians   relatives   students

1 *Most of the students in my class like rock music.*
2 *Both of my grandfathers were farmers.*
3 *One of the bands I like is U2.*
4 *Few of my friends wear high-heeled shoes.*
5
6
7
8
9

157 Complete the sentences using words from the box.

> a few (of)   all (of)   any (of)   each (of)   few (of)   half (of)   most (of)   much (of)   none (of)

1 It is widely believed that ....*all*.... human beings are descended from one common ancestor.

2 When Jill decided to sell her car, she phoned round her friends. But .... them wanted to buy it, so she put an ad in the paper.

3 Do .... your colleagues give you birthday presents?

4 When my rich uncle died, he left .... his fortune to his cat and the other half to a distant cousin! We had never expected to receive .... it, but we were disappointed that he hadn't left .... it to us.

5 I think .... children enjoy going to funfairs, although I know .... who are frightened of the big rides.

6 We'll have to work quickly because I haven't got .... time.

7 Before mixing the cake, weigh .... ingredient precisely.

8 I'll have to buy a new tie. .... the ones I've got matches this jacket.

9 .... people enjoy housework, and I'm not one of them.

10 Brett lost his wallet, so he phoned .... the shops he'd visited. But he got the same answer from .... place. Unfortunately, ... their staff had found it.

158 There are mistakes in nine of these sentences. Correct the sentences where necessary. Write 'OK' if the sentence is already correct.

1 He shouted at all of students although most of us had done nothing wrong.   ....*all of the students*....

   Can anyone use the tennis courts or only college students?   ....*OK*....

3 What happens if anybody get left behind?   ....

4 What a boring town! There are not good restaurants, nothing!   ....

5 I think he was lonely because he had a few friends and none of his neighbours ever spoke to him.   ....

6 We can't use this room because there are no chairs in it.   ....

7 I've wasted two hours because the whole information you gave me was wrong.   ....

8 When I got on the plane, the steward told me I could have some seat because there were so few passengers on the flight.   ....

9 You can't borrow money from me because I have no.   ....

10 The problem is that I have much homework to do at weekends, so I have very little time for sport.   ....

11 I don't know whether our scheme will make a profit, but any money we raise will be given to charity.   ....

12 I feel so embarrassed that all know my problem.   ....

159 Choose the correct alternative.

You can't turn the clock back

Last week I made the mistake of revisiting the village where I grew up. It used to be a small, friendly community with two farms and a number of old cottages round the village green. I realised very quickly that although in (1) <u>many / few</u> ways it appears unchanged, in reality hardly (2) <u>nothing / anything</u> is the same.

(3) <u>All / Every</u> the pretty cottages are there, of course, and (4) <u>both / most</u> the traditional farmhouses. But (5) <u>none of the / none of</u> inhabitants are country people. All of (6) <u>they / them</u> are commuters, who leave early (7) <u>every morning / all the mornings</u> for the nearby town.

(8) <u>Neither of / Neither</u> the farmhouses is attached to a farm these days; the land has been sold and is managed by (9) <u>somebody / anyone</u> in an office (10) <u>anywhere / somewhere</u> who has (11) <u>little / a little</u> interest in the village itself.

There are (12) <u>few / a few</u> new houses, but they have (13) <u>no / none of</u> local character. You can see the same style (14) <u>anywhere / somewhere</u> in the country.

(15) <u>The whole / Whole</u> of the village, in fact, has been tidied up so much that it looks (16) <u>any / no</u> more picturesque than any suburban street.

160   Can you answer the questions about the people in Box A? Use the information from Boxes B and C.

A

1 Who was Mary Seacole?
2 Who was Antonio Stradivari?
3 Who was Ibn Battuta?
4 Who was Marie Tussaud?
5 Who was Joseph Lister?
6 Who was Sirimavo Bandaranaike?
7 Who was Joseph Niepce?

Marie Tussaud

Joseph Lister

Mary Seacole

Antonio Stradivari

Ibn Battuta

Sirimavo Bandaranaike

Joseph Niepce

B

| Sri Lankan   Englishman   Frenchman   Swiss woman   Italian   Moroccan   ~~Jamaican~~ |

C

He travelled through Africa and Asia.
He made wonderful violins.
~~She worked as a nurse and saved many lives.~~
He produced the first permanent photograph.
She opened a waxworks museum.
He began the use of antiseptics in operating theatres.
She became the first woman prime minister in the world

1   *Mary Seacole was a Jamaican who worked as a nurse and saved many lives.*
2   ....
3   ....
4   ....
5   ....
6   ....
7   ....

61 Complete the conversation with **who**, **that**, **whose** or **where**.
If no word is necessary, leave the space empty (–).

Zoe and Pat are planning a party next Thursday.

ZOE: Well, who shall we ask to this party?

PAT: Oh, not too many. Just a few people (1) ....–.... we can
       be relaxed with.

ZOE: Yes, I agree. So, who, for example?

PAT: John and Jason, of course, and Carlo.

ZOE: Carlo? Who's he?

PAT: He's the Italian guy (2) ....who.... is staying with John.

ZOE: Oh, yeah. Is he the one (3) .... wallet got stolen when they were in London?

PAT: That's right. They caught the guy (4) .... took it, but he'd already spent all the
       money (5) .... Carlo had brought with him.

ZOE: Poor Carlo. Perhaps the party will cheer him up.

PAT: It might, if we ask the girl (6) .... he's been going out with.

ZOE: Who's that?

PAT: Celia's her name. She works in that cinema (7) .... they show all the new
       films.

ZOE: But will she be free on Thursday evening?

PAT: Yes, it's her evening off. That's the reason (8) .... I suggested Thursday.

ZOE: OK. Who else? What about Nicky and Cherry?

PAT: Are they the people (9) .... you went to France with?

ZOE: Yes. If they bring their boyfriends, that'll be ten of us. But have you got a room
       (10) .... is big enough? My landlady says we can't use her sitting-room
       because we made too much mess the last time (11) .... she let us have a party.

PAT: It's all right. Our house has got a basement (12) .... we store old furniture. If
       we clean it up, it'll be fine.

ZOE: Great. Let's go and have a look at it.

162 Complete the sentences with your own ideas. Use a relative pronoun.

1 I like meeting people ....who have travelled widely.. .
2 I enjoy parties ....which go on till dawn.. .
3 I avoid going to restaurants ....
4 Most of my friends are people ....
5 I never wear clothes ....
6 My favourite films are those ....
7 I feel sorry for children ....
8 My best friend is someone ....
9 I'm going to buy a cupboard ....
10 I wish I had a job ....

163   Tick (✓) the sentence which matches the situation.

1 I have three umbrellas. I bought one of them in Paris. That one needs repairing.
   a The umbrella which I bought in Paris needs repairing. ✓
   b The umbrella, which I bought in Paris, needs repairing.

2 I have one colleague. He works extremely hard. He has few friends.
   a My colleague who works extremely hard is not very popular.
   b My colleague, who works extremely hard, is not very popular. ✓

3 I have several aunts. One works in New York. She's getting married.
   a My aunt who works in New York is getting married.
   b My aunt, who works in New York, is getting married.

4 Peter made some sandwiches. They have all been eaten. You made some too. Your sandwiches
   have not been eaten.
   a The sandwiches which Peter made have all been eaten.
   b The sandwiches, which Peter made, have all been eaten.

5 There was only one park in this town. Someone has built over it. We used to play in the park
   when we were children.
   a The local park where we played as children has been built over.
   b The local park, where we played as children, has been built over.

6 One of my French teachers helps me with my homework. The other one lives too far away.
   a The French teacher whose house is near mine helps me with my homework.
   b The French teacher, whose house is near mine, helps me with my homework.

7 You met one of my cousins last summer, the one from America. He's coming to stay again.
   a My American cousin who you met last summer is coming to stay again.
   b My American cousin, who you met last summer, is coming to stay again.

8 There were a lot of candidates in the presidential election. Three of them were women. The
   winner was one of them. She had campaigned for better housing conditions.
   a The woman who had campaigned for better housing conditions has been elected President.
   b The woman, who had campaigned for better housing conditions, has been elected President.

9 I received lots of flowers when I was ill, but only my boyfriend sent me roses. I put the roses in
   my favourite vase.
   a The roses which my boyfriend sent look beautiful in my favourite vase.
   b The roses, which my boyfriend sent, look beautiful in my favourite vase.

10 I took two cameras away with me. You lent me one of them. That's the one that got broken.
   a The camera which you lent me has been broken.
   b The camera, which you lent me, has been broken.

64 Choose the correct alternative.

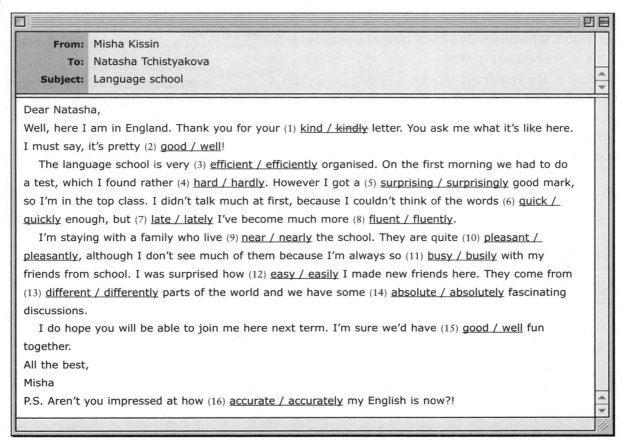

From: Misha Kissin
To: Natasha Tchistyakova
Subject: Language school

Dear Natasha,

Well, here I am in England. Thank you for your (1) <u>kind</u> / ~~kindly~~ letter. You ask me what it's like here. I must say, it's pretty (2) <u>good / well</u>!

The language school is very (3) <u>efficient / efficiently</u> organised. On the first morning we had to do a test, which I found rather (4) <u>hard / hardly</u>. However I got a (5) <u>surprising / surprisingly</u> good mark, so I'm in the top class. I didn't talk much at first, because I couldn't think of the words (6) <u>quick / quickly</u> enough, but (7) <u>late / lately</u> I've become much more (8) <u>fluent / fluently</u>.

I'm staying with a family who live (9) <u>near / nearly</u> the school. They are quite (10) <u>pleasant / pleasantly</u>, although I don't see much of them because I'm always so (11) <u>busy / busily</u> with my friends from school. I was surprised how (12) <u>easy / easily</u> I made new friends here. They come from (13) <u>different / differently</u> parts of the world and we have some (14) <u>absolute / absolutely</u> fascinating discussions.

I do hope you will be able to join me here next term. I'm sure we'd have (15) <u>good / well</u> fun together.

All the best,

Misha

P.S. Aren't you impressed at how (16) <u>accurate / accurately</u> my English is now?!

65 There are mistakes in seven of these sentences. Correct the sentences where necessary. Write 'OK' if the sentence is already correct.

1 'Please get a move on!' shouted Trevor <u>impatient</u>.   shouted Trevor impatiently

2 I believe she is a very lonely woman.   OK

3 I didn't like his plan, which seemed unnecessary complicated to me.

4 I'm sure you could win the match if you tried hardly.

5 I have an awful headache, so could you please be quiet?

6 Soraya's only been in France a year, but she speaks perfectly French.

7 The reason Bruce gets so tired is that he has an exceptional demanding job.

8 My mother was ill last year, but she's good enough to go on holiday now.

9 David ran as fast as he could, but he still arrived late.

10 Jean always says she's short of money, but I happen to know she actually has a very good-paid job.

166 A class of students is studying environmental issues with their teacher. Look at the chart and complete their conversation.

TEACHER: Who recycled (1) ....the highest.... percentage of glass in 1992?

FLORA: The Dutch did.

TEACHER: And who recycled (2) .... percentage?

WAYNE: The Greeks.

TEACHER: Right. What about the Spanish? How well did they do?

JILL: They did (3) .... the Greeks, but (4) .... the Portuguese.

TEACHER: Did the French recycle a (5) .... percentage of glass .... the Danes?

KEVIN: No, not quite. About five per cent (6) ....

TEACHER: What about the Italians?

BRONWEN: They recycled about (7) .... percentage .... the Belgians.

TEACHER: Yes. That's about five per cent (8) .... the Danes.

ALEX: But it's about ten per cent (9) .... the Germans.

TEACHER: True. Now let's go on to talk about what we're going to do next.

Could do better
Percentage of glass recycled by European countries 1992

	20	40	60
Netherlands			
Germany			
Belgium			
Italy			
Denmark			
France			
Portugal			
Spain			
Greece			

167 The class in the previous exercise took part in a paper recycling project. Look at the chart below and write sentences comparing the students' achievements.

Flora 50 kilos Kevin 45 kilos Jill 30 kilos Bronwen 30 kilos Alex 25 kilos Wayne 10 kilos

1 (Kevin / Flora / Jill)
...Kevin didn't collect as much paper as Flora, but he collected more than Jill...

2 (Alex / Bronwen / Jill) ...Alex collected five kilos less than Bronwen or Jill...

3 (Flora) ...Flora collected the most paper...

4 (Jill / Alex / Wayne) ....

5 (Bronwen / Jill) ....

6 (Wayne) ....

7 (Alex / Bronwen / Wayne) ....

8 (Jill / Flora / Alex) ....

68   Complete the conversations. Use the correct form of the word(s) given and any other words you need.

A   JOE: Why have you bought a new car?

     AMY: We needed one with a (1) __bigger__ (big) boot, to take our sports gear.

B   ANDY: Are you still trying to get that stain out of the rug?

     JENNY: Yes. I don't know what it is. I've tried all sorts of soaps and things, but it's still (2) __no cleaner than__ (clean) when I started.

C   ROSE: Do you happen to know which is (3) __the smallest planet in__ (small / planet) our solar system?

     JILL: Pluto, isn't it? I know it's (4) __the furthest__ (far) away from the sun.

D   FRED: How was your driving test?

     GEORGE: Oh, not so bad really. It was (5) .... (much / easy) I'd expected, in fact.

     FRED: So, you've passed?

     GEORGE: Yes, I have.

     FRED: Congratulations! That's (6) .... (good) news I've heard for ages!

E   MARY: Which is (7) .... (high / mountain) Africa?

     ANNE: I'm not sure. Kilimanjaro, perhaps?

     MARY: Where's that? In Zambia?

     ANNE: No, it's (8) .... (far / north) that. Kenya I think.

F   GAIL: Shall we go for a swim? It's lovely and sunny.

     MICK: I'm not sure. There's quite a strong wind. I think you'll find it's (9) .... (not / warm) it looks when you get outside.

G   EDDY: We'd better go to the bank this morning.

     SEAN: Can't we go (10) .... (late)?

     EDDY: No. They shut (11) .... (early / here) they do at home.

H   WILL: Hurry up! We'll miss the train. Can't you run (12) .... (fast)?

     PETE: Sorry, I'm going (13) .... (fast) I can already.

     WILL: OK. I guess you're quite a bit (14) .... (short / me), after all.

I   CHRIS: I hear you were having problems with your business last year. Is it (15) .... (good) this year?

     JODIE: No. I'm afraid it's (16) .... (bad) if anything.

     CHRIS: I suppose people just aren't spending (17) .... (much / money) they used to.

169 Rewrite the sentences using the words in brackets.

1 We left early.
   (the meeting) _We left the meeting early._

2 We went to the cinema and we had a meal.
   (also) ....

3 My sister plays tennis in summer.
   (in the park) ....

4 She's worked since she left school.
   (for that company) ....

5 If you order the CD on the Internet, it will be delivered by post.
   (tomorrow) ....

6 He calls on his mobile every lunchtime.
   (his girlfriend) ....

7 When you opened the box, did you find a note?
   (inside it) ....

8 We were late for work because of the traffic jam.
   (all) ....

9 I'm going to Zurich soon.
   (definitely) ....

10 The meal was lovely. My friends had asked the restaurant to make a birthday cake.
    (even) (for me) ....

170 Write three sentences about each of the three people in the left-hand column of the chart.
Use the words in each row and add the adverbs at the top.

	occasionally	usually	hardly ever
Angela	arrives at work early	isn't in the office at lunchtime	has taken a day off
John	is late for work	won't do overtime	has sandwiches for lunch
Craig	has offered to work through lunch	leaves later than everyone else	is ill

1 _Angela occasionally arrives at work early._

2 _John is occasionally late for work._

3 ....

4 ....

5 ....

6 ....

7 ....

8 ....

9 ....

71 Rewrite each <u>underlined</u> sentence using the adverb in brackets.

Andy and Jane came home from shopping on Saturday to find their house had been burgled.
A police officer has come to investigate the crime.

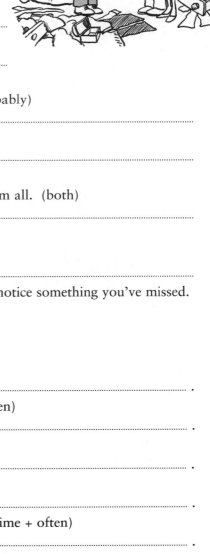

OFFICER: You say you're not sure how the thieves got in. Before I
           look round, can I ask you a few questions about the house?
ANDY: Of course.
OFFICER: (1) <u>Do you lock the front door when you go out?</u> (always)
           Do you always lock the front door when you go out?
ANDY: (2) <u>Yes, and I locked it yesterday.</u> (definitely)
           Yes, and I definitely locked it yesterday.
OFFICER: OK. What about the windows?
ANDY: (3) <u>Well, the downstairs ones are locked.</u> (always)

           ....

JANE: (4) <u>We have a lock on the little one in the hall.</u> (even)

           ....

OFFICER: And upstairs?
JANE: (5) Well, I think <u>most of the windows were locked</u>. (probably)

           ....

ANDY   (6) <u>They were locked on Friday.</u> (all)

           ....

JANE: Are you sure?
ANDY: (7) Yes, <u>I knew we would be out all day</u>, so I checked them all. (both)

           ....

OFFICER: And you didn't open any on Friday night?
ANDY: (8) No, <u>I didn't</u>. (certainly)

           ....

OFFICER: Well, I can't understand it. Let's look round. Perhaps I'll notice something you've missed.

72 Answer the questions using the words in brackets.

1 What does Timothy have for breakfast? (has an egg + usually)
  He *usually has an egg* .

2 Does Margaret watch a lot of television? (doesn't own one + even)
  She *doesn't even own one* .

3 Why did James leave the party? (was bored + probably)
  He ....

4 Does Sally like your house? (has been there + never)
  She ....

5 Do you know where Maureen might be? (has a rest about this time + often)
  She ....

6 How is Keith getting on with his homework? (has finished it + almost)
  He ....

Prepositions of time

173 Put in **at, for, during, by, until** or **in**.

The city of London was founded by the Romans (1) ....*in*.... the year 43 AD. (2) ....*During*.... the next few years it quickly became the main trading centre in Britain. (3) .... two hundred years after the Romans left, the city was almost forgotten. Its full importance did not return (4) .... the eleventh century. (5) .... the end of that century, the government of England was based in Westminster and the Tower of London had been started. (6) .... the Middle Ages London continued to grow and (7) .... the time of Shakespeare, it had become a prosperous capital city with many fine buildings. Unfortunately, most of these buildings were made of wood and (8) .... 1666 they were almost all destroyed by a fire which lasted (9) .... several days. This was a great tragedy for the people living there (10) .... that time, but it is true that many of the areas which are most attractive today were planned (11) .... the rebuilding which followed.

174 Answer the questions, beginning each answer with a preposition.

1 When's your birthday? ....
2 What year were you born? ....
3 When do you usually go shopping? ....
4 What time of the year do you go on holiday? ....
5 When do you watch TV? ....
6 When did you last drink a glass of fruit juice? ....
7 How long have you been studying English? ....

75 Put in **for, during, by, until, at** or **in**. If no word is necessary, leave the space empty (–).

THE WAY PEOPLE WORK

Eleanor is a nurse who works the night shift. How does she manage?

'Well, I finish work (1) ...*at*... 6.30 am. Then I go home, have a bath and try to be in bed (2) ...*by*... half past eight. (3) .... the same time as I'm getting ready for bed, Jeffrey, my husband, and our four-year-old daughter, Elaine, are getting up. Jeffrey takes her to nursery school, which she started (4) .... last year. I usually sleep (5) .... about three o'clock (6) .... the afternoon. I have to be at the school (7) .... 3.30 to collect Elaine. We come home and I play with her, and try to get some housework done (8) .... the same time. When my husband comes home, we eat. If I'm lucky, I can relax (9) .... an hour before putting Elaine to bed. Then I do some of the housework that didn't get done earlier. I allow plenty of time to get to the hospital because if I'm not there (10) ....

time, another nurse will have to go on working (11) .... I arrive.

I'm often very tired (12) .... the time I finish, but I don't really mind. There's a special atmosphere in the hospital (13) .... night. Of course, I have a free day (14) .... every week. And the hours suit us, (15) .... the moment anyway. I may want to work (16) .... the day when Elaine goes to a different school. Perhaps I'll be ready for a change (17) .... then.'

176 Choose the correct alternative.

A JAY: Oh, look. Here's a photo taken in my classroom at primary school. Can you recognise me (1) <u>in / on</u> it?

ANNA: No, I don't think so. Unless that's you right (2) <u>in / at</u> the back.

JAY: No, that's not me. I'm the one standing (3) <u>in / at</u> the corner.

ANNA: In trouble as usual!

B PIA: I don't understand this.

LILY: What?

PIA: Well, I want to check something with the college, but it says (4) <u>in / on</u> this letter that I must give a reference number when I phone, and I can't find it.

LILY: It's in that little booklet, (5) <u>in / on</u> the first page.

PIA: Oops! So it is. Thanks.

C MEL : Did you see Yves (6) <u>in / at</u> the disco?

JAN: No, of course not. He returned (7) <u>to / in</u> France last week.

MEL: But I'm sure I saw him (8) <u>in / on</u> the bus yesterday. In fact, he waved to me when we arrived (9) <u>to / at</u> the bus station.

JAN: How strange. We'll have to investigate what he's up to!

177 Put in on, at or in.

Dear Gordon,

Many thanks for agreeing to stay in the flat while I'm in Wales. I enclose the key and here's the list of what's where that I promised you.

If you lose this key, Mrs Johnson (1) ...*in*... the flat (2) .... the ground floor has a spare one. If she's away, the landlord lives (3) .... the building (4) .... the end of the street. It's called Laurel Villa, and the landlord is Mr Emerson. They both know you'll be there while I'm away.

The electricity and gas main switches are (5) .... the wall (6) .... the back of the large cupboard (7) .... the study. You can turn the water off by the large tap (8) .... the corner of the bathroom. I hope you won't need to!

I've made a list of all the useful phone numbers I can think of. It's stuck (9) .... the kitchen door.

I hope you have a good time.

Much love,

Shirley

Electricity and gas main switches

78 Choose the correct alternative.

TROUBLE AT NORTON MINING

The entire workforce of Norton Mining has gone (1) <u>on</u> / <del>in</del> strike following a serious accident at the mine in Coolooma in Queensland. The cause (2) <u>for / of</u> the accident is unclear, but the union is blaming management attitudes (3) <u>on / to</u> safety regulations. A spokesperson said, 'Damage (4) <u>of / to</u> equipment was frequently ignored and union demands (5) <u>for / of</u> safer working practices were rejected. The managers' relationship (6) <u>with / to</u> the union was very poor, so although we pointed out that there'd been a rise (7) <u>of / in</u> the number of minor accidents over the past year, they said there was no need (8) <u>for / of</u> a change in working practices.'

John Norton, the chairman of Norton Mining, is away (9) <u>on / in</u> a business trip. His secretary said she had spoken to him (10) <u>by / on</u> the phone. The news of the accident had come (11) <u>like / as</u> a great shock to him, she added. She was unable to say when he would be back.

It is understood that the police would like to speak to Mr Norton in connection (12) <u>with / to</u> a number of his financial dealings. ∎

79 Complete the answers. Use the words in brackets with one of the prepositions from the box and any other words you need.

as at by in like on

1 What's this room? (store room)
   We use it ….*as a store room*…. .

2 Where's Geraldine? (holiday)
   She's …*on holiday*…. .

3 What would you like to do now? (shade)
   Let's sit …………………………………………………………… .

4 Why aren't you eating any cake? (diet)
   I'm …………………………………………………………… .

5 Can you really afford to buy that CD player now? (credit card)
   It's OK. I'll pay …………………………………………………………… .

6 Was the exhibition interesting? (little-known Russian artists)
   Yes. The works were all …………………………………………………………… .

7 Why were so many people injured in the crash? (130 kilometres an hour)
   Because the train was travelling …………………………………………………………… .

8 Why are you writing so slowly? (capital letters)
   Because I have to put my address …………………………………………………………… .

9 Why is your hand so swollen? (wasp)
   I got stung …………………………………………………………… .

10 What sort of car has Christine bought this time? (the last one)
   A Ford, …………………………………………………………… .

11 What are you doing in the summer holidays? (motorcycle messenger)
   I've got a job …………………………………………………………… .

180 Complete the sentences using the prepositions from the box and your own ideas.

> about   at   for   in   of   on   to

1 I know someone who's brilliant _at playing the saxophone_ .
2 It's difficult to feel sorry ....
3 Scientists are always looking ....
4 My neighbours are usually friendly ....
5 Football fans feel proud ....
6 Not many people are interested ....
7 Not enough people are prepared to do something ....
8 Many children are nervous ....
9 Everyone in the world has heard ....
10 My mood depends ....
11 I enjoy laughing ....
12 I sometimes take photos ....
13 Lots of children believe ....
14 I'm no good ....

181 Match the beginning of each sentence with the most suitable ending.

1 Jake hasn't forgiven Helen	*a* on him to help her.	1 ___d___
2 He thought she relied	*b* about what he thinks.	2 ....
3 He'll never succeed	*c* after herself.	3 ....
4 She no longer cares	*d* ~~for going away without him.~~	4 ....
5 She's old enough to look	*e* of managing alone.	5 ....
6 She's perfectly capable	*f* in changing her opinion.	6 ....
7 His shirt is similar	*g* with his present.	7 ....
8 My brother was pleased	*h* at remembering names.	8 ....
9 I'm completely hopeless	*i* to one I've got.	9 ....

182 Match the beginning of each sentence with the most suitable preposition. Then use your own ideas to complete the sentence.

1 The lorry collided	1 ___b___	*a* of ....
2 The bus crashed	2	*b* with _a car_ .
3 The square was full	3	*c* from ....
4 The minibus belonged	4	*d* on ....
5 They borrowed the car	5	*e* into ....
6 They blamed the accident	6	*f* to ....
7 The owner was upset	7	*g* for ....
8 The driver apologised	8	*h* about ....

83 Write a sentence for each picture. Use **going to** + a phrasal verb.

1
She __'s going to knock them over__ .

2
He _____ .

3
He _____ .

4
He _____ .

5
She _____ .

6
He _____ .

7
They _____ .

8
She _____ .

184 Complete each sentence with a preposition.

1 I'm looking forward ...*to*... seeing my cousin.
2 My uncle ran away .... home when he was small.
3 Have you ever fallen out .... anyone?
4 How well do you get on .... your colleagues?
5 My sister is on a diet, so she's cut down .... chocolate.
6 We went up .... a woman and asked her for directions.
7 My brother pointed his old girlfriend out .... me as she came into the restaurant.
8 The new manager came up .... several interesting suggestions.
9 I'll get back .... you as soon as I've got any news.
10 My brother gets away .... all sorts of things I wouldn't be allowed to do.

185 Complete each sentence with the correct form of **get** + one of the words from the box. Use one of the words twice.

| away   back   by   in   on   out |

1 The taxi stopped and a small boy ...*got out*..., holding a bunch of flowers.
2 We haven't had a holiday yet this year. We've been too busy to ....
3 What time do you think you'll .... here from the theatre?
4 With that enormous hole in the roof, there's no way we can stop the rain .... if there's a storm.
5 It's natural for parents to worry about how their children .... when they're away from home.
6 Modern buses are designed to make it easier for passengers to ....
7 I don't earn much, but I try to .... without borrowing.

186 Complete each sentence with the correct form of **take** + one of the words from the box. Use two of the words twice.

| away   down   in   off   up |

1 The woman ...*took off*... her jacket and began work.
2 I had to pay £100 to have my old car ....
3 Few of the criminals .... by the policeman's attempt to disguise himself as a beggar.
4 The students were told to .... the posters which they had hung from their windows.
5 We .... jazz dance last year in the hope of losing some weight.
6 I can't keep my motorbike in the garage because the car .... all the space.
7 We were offered drinks soon after the plane ....

187 Complete each sentence with the correct form of **go** + one of the words from the box. Use one of the words twice.

> away   back   in   on   off   out

1 I know the house isn't empty because I saw a man .....*go in*.... about an hour ago.
2 We know the group has cancelled their concert, but no-one really knows what
   ....
3 We heard that someone had put a bomb in the shopping centre, but luckily it failed to
   ....
4 He was born in Scotland, but it's unlikely he .... to live there as he's been
   in London so long.
5 I'm sorry, you can't see the manager because he .... on business for a few
   days.
6 The little green light on the front of my computer .... Does it matter?
7 If you phone after midday, call my mobile because I .... for a walk.

188 Complete each sentence with the correct form of **put** + one of the words from the box. Use one of the words three times.

> back   down   off   on   out

1 One fire officer was slightly injured while ....*putting out*.... the fire in the hotel.
2 After work, I like to .... some old clothes and do a bit of gardening.
3 After cleaning, the paintings must .... in exactly the same places on the wall.
4 Is it OK to .... the television, or will it disturb you?
5 We'll have to .... the barbecue till another day if the weather doesn't improve.
6 Please .... that suitcase. It's much too heavy for you to carry.
7 It's cold in here. Shall I .... the central heating?

189 Complete each sentence with the correct form of **turn** + one of the words from the box. Use two of the words twice.

> down   off   on   out   up

1 I always ....*turn on*.... the computer as soon as I get home.
2 We didn't expect good weather yesterday, but it .... quite warm.
3 I hadn't seen him since we were students, then one day he .... and asked
   me to have lunch with him.
4 We weren't aware of it, but it .... that we went to the same university.
5 Can you .... the heater? I'm freezing!
6 If you .... the engine, we'll be able to hear the waves and the seabirds.
7 Go and tell your brother to .... his stereo. It's far too loud.

190 Complete the announcement with the verbs from the box in the correct form and the words in brackets.

cross out	fill in	hand back	~~hand out~~
hold up	leave out	rub out	tear up

'Ladies and gentlemen, we will arrive at our next destination in three hours. At this port some passengers will need visas. In a few minutes members of the crew (1) *will hand out landing cards* (landing cards). Please read the card carefully to check whether you need to (2) .... (it). If you do not need the card, please (3) .... (not / it), but (4) .... (it) immediately to the crew member. When completing the card, be careful not to (5) .... (any information). If you make a mistake, (6) .... (it) neatly. Please do not try to (7) .... (it) with an eraser. Failure to complete the form correctly will result in our whole group (8) .... at the immigration office, so please read through what you have written. Thank you.'

191 Complete the newspaper article with the verbs from the box in the correct form and the words in brackets.

break down	bring up	fall out with	find out	keep away
let down	put up with	run away from	show off	~~split up~~

STAR ADMITS HEARTBREAK

Happier days

Friends of TV celebrity couple Rosie and Jeff have confirmed that they (1) *are splitting up* . They say Rosie (2) .... that Jeff is seeing another woman. 'The relationship (3) .... ,' revealed a tearful Rosie. 'I'm not prepared to (4) .... him any longer,' she added. 'He (5) .... in nightclubs and he (6) .... (me) in front of my friends.'

Rosie plans to (7) .... (their daughter Mimi) on her own, but she (8) .... (not / her) from Jeff. 'Just because we (9) .... each other, it doesn't mean he can (10) .... his responsibilities to Mimi,' she said.

92 Complete the newspaper article with the verbs from the box in the correct form and the words in brackets.

| bring up | close down | do up | hold up | pay back | rip off | ~~set up~~ |

Last call for Hi! Electronics

Talks are being held with employees of Hi! Electronics, the firm which (1) _was set up_ by Anthony Highbridge only two years ago with a £5m loan. His bank says he must (2) .... (it) this month or his business will have to (3) .... Customers have claimed that Highbridge (4) .... (them) with poor goods and inefficient service. Mr Highbridge stated yesterday that his problems began because his business development plans (5) .... by the bank.

'Our shop was old-fashioned and I needed an extra loan so that we could (6) .... (it). But every time I (7) .... (the subject), the bank said I had to wait.'

93 Complete the newspaper article with the verbs from the box in the correct form.

| blow up | ~~break down~~ | drive away | drop off | give up | go off | go on | ride off |

NOISES IN THE NIGHT

Residents of Victoria Street in Thornton were disturbed last night by an unusual accident. At eleven o'clock a car (1) _broke down_ near the end of the street and the driver left his vehicle there while he (2) .... with his journey by taxi. An hour later, the car's alarm (3) .... when it was hit by a stolen van. The engine of the van (4) .... , so the thief tried to (5) .... in the car. But he (6) .... when the car wouldn't start and stole a bicycle instead.

'I (7) .... to sleep at about midnight,' said Michael Patel who lives at 11 Victoria Street, 'then I was woken by a terrible ringing and a loud bang. When I looked out of my window, I saw a man (8) .... on my bicycle!'

194 Rewrite the sentences replacing the <u>underlined</u> verbs with the verbs from the box in the correct form.

carry on	come back	cut down	find out	leave out	~~look back on~~	plug in
put off	put up with	try out	turn down	work out		

1 I'm sure we'll all <u>remember</u> this holiday with great pleasure.
   I'm sure we'll all look back on this holiday with great pleasure.

2 She promised to <u>return</u> at the end of the summer, but he never saw her again.

3 He <u>calculated</u> that it would cost $50,000 to do a degree in the States.

4 This lead should be <u>connected</u> to the back of your computer.

5 You have <u>omitted</u> several important facts in your report.

6 We can't <u>continue</u> if you won't co-operate.

7 We can <u>test</u> this sound system in the shop before we buy it.

8 He was offered a new job, but he <u>refused</u> it because he didn't want to move house.

9 We moved house because we couldn't <u>bear</u> the noise from the motorway any longer.

10 He had to leave when his boss <u>discovered</u> what he had been doing.

11 Potential customers <u>were discouraged</u> by the difficulty of parking near the restaurant.

12 The company has succeeded in <u>reducing</u> the amount of packaging used by twenty-five per cent.

195 Rewrite this extract from a letter using the verbs from the box in the correct form.

come up with	drop out of	get away with	~~get out of~~	put up with

My cousin Ruth is really lazy. She always tries to <u>avoid</u> studying.   *get out of*
She used to invent all kinds of excuses when she was younger.
Now she's left college without finishing her course. Her father
says he won't tolerate her behaviour any longer, but I bet Ruth
won't be punished for it, as usual.

196 Complete the sentences with suitable verbs in the correct form.

1 If you're offered the job, surely you won't .... it down?

2 Never .... off until tomorrow what you can do today.

3 The departure of the plane .... up by poor weather.

4 I .... out the mistake and wrote the correct word.

5 The children loved their aunt, who .... them up.

6 The company blamed the mistake on their suppliers, who .... them down.

7 I'm no good at .... up stories, but I'll read you one if you like.

8 A cat got into the museum and .... off the burglar alarm.

197 Complete each answer with a suitable phrasal verb + a pronoun if necessary.

1 NINA: What shall I do with this form?

  JOHN: Just ....*fill it in*.... and send it to the address at the top.

2 FRED: Is Sonia a fast runner?

  SUE: Oh, yes. Nobody else on the team can ....

3 ALAN: Why didn't you buy a dictionary?

  DAVE: The bookshop has ....

4 MAY: Did you believe Nicola's story?

  EVAN: No, I knew she must have ....

5 GREG: Do we need to finish this drawing before the meeting?

  BILL: Yes, so you'd better ....

6 CILLA: What are the girls doing in the garden with the tent?

  ALEC: They want to .... before they go away, to check that it's OK.

7 LEE: Were you disappointed that Graham didn't keep his promise?

  RUTH: Yes, we all felt he'd .... rather badly.

8 IAN: Did Francesca play with her cousins when they came to stay?

  JIM: Oh, yes. She .... very well.

198 Complete the sentences with your own ideas. Use **on** or **off**.

1 I turned ...*on the computer and checked my email*.. .

2 The children set ....

3 The lazy student put ....

4 I tried ....

5 We took ....

6 The girl switched ....

7 The old ladies carried ....

8 The tour guide walked ....

199 Complete the sentences with your own ideas. Use **up** or **down**.

1 The young businessman set ....
2 My boyfriend turned ....
3 The old lady put ....
4 My grandfather took ....
5 The workmen knocked ....
6 The gangsters beat ....
7 The young couple were saving ....
8 The business closed ....

200 Complete the sentences with your own ideas. Use **in** or **out**.

1 We often eat ....
2 The prisoner climbed ....
3 The new student joined ....
4 Air travellers must check ....
5 The picture has been cut ....
6 The schoolboy let ....
7 My secretary will sort ....
8 The investigation was carried ....

Solution to Exercise 143

9.05   Lucy left the study.
        Trevor phoned Gerald.
9.15   Lucy saw Gerald on the phone.
        Dorothy and Doctor Emerson heard Trevor shouting at Gerald, on the phone. When
        he was checking the accounts, he discovered that Gerald had been stealing from the
        business.
9.25   Doctor Emerson left, banging the front door.
9.30   Gerald entered the house and killed Trevor after a short argument.
9.40   Gerald left the house and met Lucy on her way home.

Key

1

2 're singing / are singing
3 's playing / is playing
4 're holding / are holding
5 're offering / are offering
6 's organising / is organising

2

2 'm meeting / am meeting
3 Is my radio disturbing
4 'm enjoying / am enjoying
5 Is anyone using
6 're having / are having
7 are those people shouting
8 're demonstrating / are demonstrating
9 Are you applying
10 'm considering / am considering
11 Is Jane leaving
12 's flying / is flying
13 Are you coming
14 'm working / am working

3

2 's standing / is standing
3 aren't looking / are not looking
4 's wearing / is wearing
5 isn't wearing / is not wearing
6 's watching / is watching
7 's shining / is shining
8 is hanging
9 's lying / is lying

4

Students' own answers. See Exercise 3 for model answer.

5

2 passes
3 takes
4 lasts
5 don't sing
6 keep
7 doesn't happen
8 enjoy
9 don't remember
10 occurs
11 falls
12 looks
13 comes

6

2 does the post come
3 Does your sister have
4 do you see
5 do you travel
6 does your secretary keep
7 Do you want
8 do you work
9 do you spend
10 Does the paper shop sell

7

2 doesn't start
3 I'm taking
4 I'm staying
5 own
6 I drive
7 I'm making
8 I think
9 I understand
10 I help
11 he's working
12 he needs
13 I like
14 I'm learning
15 Are you coming
16 I'm spending
17 want
18 It gets
19 you decide
20 you're doing

8

Example answers:

4 My father is working in Poland this year.
5 My wife goes to the gym every week.
6 Several of my colleagues are learning English at the moment.
7 Our next-door neighbour is building a garage this year.
8 Our children go to bed late at weekends.
9 I'm working hard this term.
10 My best friend is waiting for me right now.

9

2 don't know
3 are trying
4 is getting
5 are disappearing
6 aren't doing
7 enjoy
8 consist
9 melt
10 believe
11 are already rising

10

2 *Both*
3 Are you enjoying your meal?
4 I'm thinking of selling my car.
5 *Both*
6 I don't believe his story.
7 The students seem tired today.
8 He weighs 80 kilos.
9 How often do you play tennis?
10 My brother is looking for a new job.

11

2 had
3 visited
4 discussed
5 wasn't / was not
6 drove
7 met
8 looked
9 went
10 invited
11 wasn't / was not
12 caught

12

See Exercise 11 for model answer.

13

3 While he was walking in the mountains, Henry saw a bear.
4 The students were playing a game when the professor arrived.
5 Felix phoned the fire brigade when the cooker caught fire.
6 When the starter fired his pistol, the race began.
7 I was walking home when it started to snow.
8 Andy came out of the restaurant when he saw Jenny.

14

2 built
3 wasn't selling
4 joined
5 read
6 was waiting
7 noticed
8 was playing
9 was approaching
10 ran
11 grabbed
12 offered
13 was having
14 had
15 left
16 went on

15

2 was travelling	11 thought
3 were touring	12 was trying
4 stopped	13 was
5 were shopping	14 belonged
6 went	15 was packing
7 was looking	16 chatted
8 came	17 asked
9 started	18 got married
10 called	

16

2 gave
3 was passing
4 heard
5 banged
6 invited
7 was organising *or* organised
8 refused
9 was preparing
10 passed
11 went
12 met
13 was studying
14 had
15 worked
16 were serving
17 announced
18 persuaded
19 was
20 were
21 earned
22 decided

17

Example answers:
2 I was walking home when it started to rain. I caught the bus.
3 Everyone was dancing when the lights went out. They tried to find the light switch.
4 When we came out of the cinema, the sun was shining. We decided to go for a walk.

18

2 I'm looking	10 We want
3 Do you want	11 did
4 are getting	12 lent
5 did you decide	13 managed
6 were staying	14 we choose
7 we're trying	15 gave
8 aren't looking	16 was looking
9 don't have	

19

2 didn't understand
3 tastes
4 believed
5 doesn't belong
6 are you wearing
7 was jogging
8 contained
9 Do you see
10 prefer
11 were watching

20

3 because the engineer **didn't call** for help
4 *OK*
5 **Is** her health **improving**?
6 I completely **agree** with you.
7 What **did you do** after you left school?
8 *OK*
9 why you **believed** all those stories
10 Martin **was looking** forward to
11 *OK*
12 Where **do you keep** the paper towels?

21

Example answers:
2 'm beginning / am beginning
3 hurts *or* aches
4 walk *or* go
5 visited *or* saw
6 are spending
7 walked *or* got
8 was coming *or* was walking
9 began *or* started
10 'm being / am being
11 managed
12 were looking
13 like *or* want
14 'm feeling *or* feel
15 get

22

2 do you clean
3 did you pass
4 Are you watching
5 did you go
6 Do you think
7 were you doing
8 does the post office open

23

2 've already done / have already done
3 've only been / have only been
4 haven't slept
5 've visited / have visited
6 've seen / have seen
7 've eaten / have eaten
8 've ridden / have ridden
9 've travelled / have travelled
10 haven't spent
11 haven't cashed
12 's paid / has paid
13 've had / have had

24

2 c   3 b   4 a   5 b   6 c

25

2 've been coming / have been coming *or* 've come / have come
3 've been driving / have been driving
4 've never had / have never had
5 've always been / have always been
6 've had / have had
7 've done / have done
8 've been doing / have been doing
9 've looked / have looked *or* 've been looking / have been looking
10 haven't found

26

2 *Both*
3 *Both*
4 I've known her for two years.
5 He's been very helpful.
6 *Both*
7 They've seen this film before.
8 *Both*
9 We've realised where we are now.
10 It's belonged to us for many years.
11 *Both*
12 You've broken my pen.

27

2 I've forgotten / I have forgotten
3 Have you had
4 Have you been playing about
5 Have you been studying

6 You've never asked / You have never asked

7 he's failed / he has failed … He hasn't been working

8 He's been repairing / He has been repairing

9 It's been sitting / It has been sitting

10 I've been doing / I have been doing

11 I've lost / I have lost

12 You've been grumbling / You have been grumbling

13 she's been spending / she has been spending … She's bought / She has bought … she's moved / she has moved … She's been giving / She has been giving

28

2 's gone / has gone to New York

3 've had / have had my hair done or 've been / have been to the hairdresser

4 've been / have been chopping onions

5 've sold / have sold my car

6 've cut / have cut my finger

7 've been / have been playing (football)

8 've been / have been going to dancing school or 've been / have been having lessons

29

2 haven't really enjoyed myself

3 hasn't seen his brother

4 gone

5 since you learnt/learned

6 been swimming since

7 since you tidied

8 been looking for

9 haven't been

10 hasn't had

30

Example answers:

3 I've been working from home for several years.

4 I've had a cold since yesterday.

5 When I was a child, I went swimming every day.

6 I started this exercise ten minutes ago.

7 It's three weeks since I saw my girlfriend.

8 For the past three weeks she's been working abroad.

9 I left school in 2001.

10 I've been feeling cold since I came into this room.

11 Last December I passed my driving test.

12 I haven't felt well since I got up this morning.

31

2 I've been revising

3 who's been looking

4 He's offered

5 I've been looking

6 He's designed

7 he doesn't have

8 he needs

9 He's been looking

10 I've been telling

11 He looks

12 He's coming

13 Are you spending

14 I come

15 I've been

16 Are you enjoying

17 I own

32

2 don't want … 've had / have had

3 's been suffering / has been suffering … 's seen / has seen

4 don't know … hasn't spoken

5 are you staring … haven't seen

6 'm staying / am staying … haven't been … 's lived / has lived or 's been living / has been living

7 Have you been waiting

8 've been watching / have been watching

33

2 've been / have been

3 want or plan or 're planning / are planning or 've decided / have decided

4 're enjoying / are enjoying or 've been enjoying / have been enjoying

5 've visited / have visited

6 've been walking / have been walking

7 'm writing / am writing

8 haven't bought

9 've had / have had

10 's been / has been

11 say

12 rains

13 've been / have been or 've come / have come

14 guess or suppose

34

2 we've been or we have been

3 what's causing or what is causing

4 we've been practising / we have been practising or we've practised / we have practised

5 that's really made or that really makes

6 we always win

7 we don't practise

8 We're playing / We are playing or We play

9 everyone agrees

10 we haven't practised

11 you have

12 who's been playing / who has been playing

13 He usually scores

14 he's been arriving / he has been arriving

15 he refuses

16 I say

17 he doesn't listen

18 I don't like

19 I hope

35

2 **I have lived** here ever since or **I have been living** here ever since

3 I left school **three years ago** and

4 since then I **have had** several jobs

5 For the past six months I **have been working** in Halls Department Store.

6 The manager **has said** that he is willing

7 I **have also been learning** German

36

Example answer:

Dear Ms Sparks,

I would like to apply for the job in your shop which I have seen advertised in the paper.

I am seventeen years old. My first language is Italian, but I also speak quite good German and English. I have not yet left school, but I have some experience in working in a shop as I sometimes help my uncle who runs a small supermarket.

My class teacher, Mr Pallini, has said that he is willing to give me a reference.

I hope you will consider my application.

Yours sincerely,

37

2 d   3 b   4 f   5 a   6 g   7 e

38

2 did you study ... qualified
3 did you first meet
4 you've cooked
5 wanted ... weren't
6 has happened ... We've been waiting ... he hasn't phoned
7 I posted ... haven't received
8 I've been working ... I never realised

39

2 went
3 's been / has been
4 opened
5 has Neil had
6 Has Tina spoken
7 've broken / have broken
8 told
9 've forgotten / have forgotten
10 earned
11 Did Brian give
12 's offered / has offered

40

2 has seen
3 took
4 spent
5 have become
6 were
7 has enabled

8 has really improved
9 disappeared
10 took
11 have become
12 haven't done / have not done
13 has brought
14 has solved

41

2 have you been
3 did you do *or* was the
4 did you need
5 did you want
6 have you been to *or* have you visited
7 did you stay
8 Have you brought *or* Did you bring
9 did you do
10 Did you do *or* Did you paint
11 did you become

42

Example answers:

2 Yesterday I rode my bicycle to the shops.
3 In the past six months I've done the washing up every day.
4 Since my last birthday I haven't eaten any birthday cake.
5 I haven't driven a car recently.
6 Last year I broke my leg.
7 Six months ago I passed an important exam.
8 I sucked my thumb when I was a child.
9 I didn't play tennis yesterday evening.
10 This week I've watched television every evening.

43

2 had prepared
3 arrived
4 discovered
5 had reserved
6 didn't have
7 had given
8 had also misunderstood
9 wanted
10 suspected
11 had lost

44

2 the play **had ended**
3 they **hadn't brought** any money
4 Gary **had** his laptop
5 I **found** that a thief
6 they **had mixed up** the results
7 I **hadn't seen** her
8 we **decided** to go

45

Example answers:

2 'd won the lottery / had won the lottery
3 'd gone out / had gone out
4 'd cut his hand / had cut his hand
5 'd been eating sweets / had been eating sweets
6 'd been buying a magazine / had been buying a magazine
7 'd broken her leg / had broken her leg
8 'd been stealing money / had been stealing money *or* 'd stolen / had stolen

46

2 We'd arranged / We had arranged
3 didn't you come
4 I was
5 I'd been waiting / I had been waiting
6 Didn't you get
7 I left
8 I was going
9 I noticed
10 they'd changed / they had changed
11 I put
12 I didn't find
13 I was waiting
14 I was worrying
15 what had happened
16 I saw
17 You were laughing
18 I realised
19 you'd been sitting / you had been sitting
20 I lost
21 My sister saw
22 She's been singing / She has been singing

47

Example answers:

2 I didn't use to like jazz.
3 I used to enjoy my work.
4 My sister used to be slimmer.
5 I didn't use to like air travel.
6 My brother used to have long hair.
7 I used to smoke.
8 My parents used to live in Africa.
9 My uncle used to be a swimming champion.
10 We didn't use to have a car.

48

2 found
3 used to wear
4 Did people really use to think
5 admitted
6 often used to fall
7 were
8 was planning
9 was wearing

49

3 My girlfriend **had** a dog → used to have
4 *No change*
5 there **was** a football pitch here → used to be
6 bread **didn't taste** like cardboard → didn't use to taste
7 seabirds which **followed** the ship → used to follow
8 *No change*
9 The music in this club **was** very boring → used to be
10 I **spent** a lot of time ... my sister **didn't help** at all → used to spend ... didn't use to help
11 *No change*

50

Example answers:

3 I used to watch television every day after school.
4 I used to go to the cinema every weekend, but I don't have time now.
5 I didn't use to have so much homework at my last school.

6 I didn't use to eat in restaurants, but now I go several times a week.
7 I used to listen to music while I was working, but my radio broke.
8 I used to see my grandparents every week when I was younger.

51

Example answers:

2 didn't use to be
3 had
4 used to stay
5 was talking
6 fell
7 learnt/learned ... was working
8 used to live

52

2 were
3 Do you know
4 used to cycle
5 was studying
6 did you hear
7 phoned
8 was checking
9 rang
10 told
11 Had you been expecting
12 Have you emailed
13 has been waiting

53

2 did you visit ... you were
3 haven't paid ... do I owe
4 discovered ... 'd left / had left
5 's happened / has happened ... 's lost / has lost
6 had ... 've been sorting / have been sorting
7 spent ... missed *or* 'd missed / had missed ... were
8 've always wanted / have always wanted ... have ... 've decided / have decided
9 went ...'d arrived / had arrived ... was
10 's having / is having

54

2 that only lasts
3 I'll get
4 does your evening class finish
5 Shall I come

6 I'm meeting
7 will you talk
8 he won't let
9 I'm playing
10 I'll try
11 he'll agree

55

2 're working / are working
3 will let
4 includes
5 will be
6 'm seeing / am seeing
7 'll come / will come

56

2 I'll collect
3 I'll have to
4 there will probably be
5 a local student is coming
6 We'll be able to
7 the conference doesn't start
8 they're emailing
9 I'll read
10 I'll be

57

Example answers:

3 Next summer I'm visiting my cousins in Sardinia.
4 When I finish this exercise, I'll be happy.
5 Tomorrow evening I expect I'll eat out with my friends.
6 At the end of my course I'll probably speak quite good English.
7 My next class begins at six o'clock.
8 Next week we're having a class party.
9 My course finishes on 30th May.

58

2 I won't be late.
3 I'll deliver the goods on Friday.
4 Shall we go to the swimming pool?
5 Will you stop fighting!
6 The door won't open.
7 Shall I phone for an ambulance? *or* I'll phone for an ambulance.
8 I won't pay for the goods until I've checked that they aren't damaged.

59

2 It's going to rain very soon.
3 He's going to be in trouble.
4 Who's going to help me tidy up?
5 They're going to buy a tent.
6 I'm not going to come to this restaurant again.
7 I'm going to walk to work from now on.
8 I'm going to have an early night.
9 How are we going to get home?
10 I'm going to buy petrol tonight.
11 They're going to travel to Prague by train.
12 Is she going to buy a new one?

60

2 won't do
3 I'm going to go
4 Will you hold
5 they're going to raise
6 won't start
7 I'm going to start
8 I'll cook
9 they won't change
10 Shall we eat
11 He's going to buy
12 I'm going to go

61

3 people will come
4 I'll phone
5 Shall I phone
6 I'm going to see
7 Will he give
8 We're going to advertise
9 The bank will lend
10 We'll do
11 he'll help

62

Example answers:
3 will I
4 I'll send
5 I'm going to visit
6 I'll give
7 Will
8 I'll go
9 Will you wash
10 I won't

63

Example answers:
2 I'm going to the doctor's.

3 I'll pay you back at the weekend.
4 Why won't you tell me?
5 I'm not going to fail again.
6 Will you please turn the volume down?
7 I'm going to be in a film.
8 Where are you going (to go) for your honeymoon?

64

3 I'm meeting
4 I'll make
5 finishes
6 Shall I bring
7 I'm going to try
8 you get
9 I probably won't have
10 my course starts
11 I arrive
12 I'm spending *or* I'm going to spend
13 you'll be doing
14 I'll be getting
15 I'll phone

65

2 could go
3 was able to get
4 haven't been able to find
5 could be
6 couldn't
7 could have been
8 were able to climb
9 could have cooked
10 could have been

66

2 was able to
3 couldn't *or* wasn't able to
4 was able to
5 couldn't
6 was able to
7 couldn't *or* weren't able to
8 could
9 could
10 was able to

67

3 He might have slept badly last night.
4 She might have dropped something.
5 It might be under the bed.
6 They might be planning a surprise.

7 He might have had some bad news.
8 She might be working at home.
9 She might have felt tired. *or* She might have been feeling tired.
You can use may *instead of* might *in all these sentences.*

68

Example answers:
3 you might get lost
4 you might miss the train
5 you might get fat
6 you might be tired tomorrow
7 it might break down
8 you might fail it
9 your boss might get angry
10 you might get spots
You can use may *instead of* might *in all these sentences.*

69

2 c   3 f   4 e   5 a
6 b   7 h   8 i   9 g

70

2 could have fallen
3 may have found
4 may not have done
5 couldn't have left
6 could be coming
7 may be visiting
8 may be seeing

71

2 must have been
3 can't be
4 can't be using
5 may be having
6 can't have enjoyed
7 may be delivering
8 can't have been concentrating
9 must be

72

Example answers:
3 might be
4 can't be
5 might be in
6 must have been
7 might not have seen
8 can't have told
9 might be something you

73
2 d 3 a 4 f 5 e 6 g 7 b

74
2 should have sent
3 ought to
4 don't have to
5 needn't have bothered
6 must have gone
7 should be
8 must have missed

75
2 needn't   6 mustn't
3 Shouldn't   7 should
4 shouldn't   8 needn't
5 needn't

76
2 should get the contract
3 don't have to spend a long
   time at the museum if it's not
   interesting or needn't / don't
   need to spend …
4 shouldn't have spoken to my
   mother like that
5 should have phoned me
6 needn't have made
7 mustn't find out what I've done
8 should move house now
9 didn't have to call a taxi or
   didn't need to call a taxi
10 should check the timetable
   before we leave

77
2 needn't   5 shouldn't
3 must   6 should
4 should   7 mustn't

78
1 shouldn't   4 shouldn't
2 needn't   5 should
3 should   6 must

79
2 ought to go and see her
3 ought to have visited me
4 ought not to have used it
5 ought to pick the fruit
6 ought not to be playing with a
   box of matches
7 ought to be an instruction leaflet
8 ought to have phoned her

80
2 'd better / had better
3 should
4 'd better / had better
5 'd better / had better
6 should
7 'd better / had better
8 should
9 should
10 'd better / had better

81
2 'd better / had better or
   should
3 have to
4 have to
5 'd better / had better or
   should
6 should
7 have to
8 'd better not / had better not
   or shouldn't
9 have to
10 should
11 'd better / had better or should

82
2 should check that all the windows
   are shut whenever you go out
3 shouldn't borrow money from
   people you hardly know
4 'd better / should keep the door
   shut in case someone sees us
5 have to train regularly if you
   want to succeed in athletics
6 'd better not / shouldn't wear
   that bracelet in the street. It
   might get stolen
7 'd better / should pick those
   tomatoes before they get too ripe
8 don't have to pay extra for
   delivery

83
2 a, b, c   5 a, b
3 a, b   6 a, b, c
4 b, c

84
2 he recommended (that) **I
   should try** or **I try** or **trying**
   the tourist information office
3 OK
4 **I should do** with them or
   I do with them?

5 OK (*wouldn't* would also be
   possible)
6 Should **I be** out
7 OK
8 demand **that Colin paid** or
   that Colin pay or **that Colin
   should pay** you

85
2 they should disappear
3 I search
4 he sees
5 I shouldn't bother
6 I find
7 should anyone call
8 we wait
9 we wait
10 he's

86
Example answers:
2 set my alarm last night
3 land safely
4 stay at home
5 make promises they can't keep
6 look for another
7 very difficult
8 missed the train
9 join a sports club
10 sell our car
11 got lost in the post
12 get to a garage
13 ride a horse … drive a car
14 go home

87
Example answers:
1 leave before 2 o'clock
2 arrive by 8.30
3 use your mobile in the office
4 ask permission to leave early
5 wear smart clothes
6 work on Sundays

88
2 he doesn't arrive
3 won't refund
4 you reach
5 will you cut
6 Would you work
7 didn't complain
8 Wouldn't my friends be

89

Example answers:
2 much would you earn
3 Would it help
4 will you do
5 make would you buy
6 will happen

90

2 he didn't like
3 You'll find
4 Wouldn't your parents be proud
5 I don't revise
6 would you look for
7 she wasn't/weren't
8 would you feel
9 you could

91

2 If you could find / found a job abroad, would you take it?
3 If it were/was somewhere I want/wanted to go, I'd certainly consider it carefully.
4 I'd only consider that if I were/was sure about the family.
5 If they didn't treat me well, I'd be very miserable.
6 You'd have to be sure to use a good agency. *or* You have to be sure …
7 I'll find you the address of it if you're interested.
8 If I decided to apply to an agency, would you help me write a letter? *or* If I decide to apply to an agency, will you help me write a letter?

92

Example answers:
2 What would you do if you won a lottery prize?
3 What would you do if you saw someone being mugged?
4 What would you do if your house was on fire?
5 What would you do if you were having a problem with grammar?
6 How would your brother react if you crashed his car?
7 What would happen if your teacher stepped on a banana skin?

8 What would happen if you overslept?
9 What would you and your friends do if you didn't have to earn money?
10 What would happen to car manufacturers if we all rode bicycles?
11 What would happen if all the politicians retired?
12 What would you do if you felt ill when you woke up?

93

Your answers should have the same structures as those in Exercise 92.

94

2 f   3 a   4 b   5 g   6 c   7 d

95

Example answers:
2 'd find / would find … had … were/was … 'd want / would want
3 'd known / had known … wouldn't have asked
4 wouldn't have hurt … 'd been looking / had been looking
5 love me … were/was … lost … would you do

96

Example answers:
2 If Cherry hadn't cancelled so late, the travel company would have given her a refund.
3 If the travel agent hadn't failed his final exams when he was a student, he wouldn't have felt sorry for Cherry.
4 If he hadn't had a cancellation on a tour which started later in the summer, he wouldn't have been able to transfer her booking.
5 If the booking hadn't been transferred, her father's money would have been wasted.
6 If they hadn't had a row, his girlfriend would have been with him.
7 If they hadn't been the only ones travelling alone, they wouldn't have found themselves going round the sights together.

8 If he had read about the places they were visiting, she wouldn't have spent most of her time telling him about them.
9 If she hadn't failed that exam, she wouldn't have met her future husband.

97

Example answers:
3 If I'd come home earlier, I wouldn't be so tired.
4 If I'd had some breakfast, I'd be able to concentrate.
5 If I'd remembered to book seats last week, we could go to the concert. *or* … could have gone to the concert.
6 If I hadn't missed the bus, I wouldn't have been fired.
7 If I hadn't broken my leg (when I went skiing), I could go to the wedding. *or* … could have gone to the wedding.
8 If we'd stopped to buy some petrol, we wouldn't have run out.

98

Example answers:
2 weren't/wasn't shy
3 wouldn't have seen the match
4 hadn't eaten too much
5 would be more popular
6 apologise
7 pressed this button
8 wouldn't have lost his job
9 had entered
10 had borrowed their bikes

99

4 had … would take more exercise
5 didn't leave their cars unlocked … wouldn't be so easy for thieves
6 had realised that smoking was dangerous when they were young … wouldn't have serious health problems
7 would have grown … hadn't forgotten to water them *or* had watered them
8 don't protect wildlife now … will be nothing left
9 realised the importance of energy conservation … would do

100

2 I wish I had a car.
3 I wish I worked in an office.
4 I wish I lived with my son.
5 I wish I could swim.
6 I wish I didn't live in a city.
7 I wish I were/was a helicopter pilot.
8 I wish I didn't have short hair.

101

Example answers:
Martin:
I wish he'd wash his coffee cup.
I wish he wouldn't leave dirty clothes around the room.
I wish he wouldn't come in late.
I wish he wouldn't lie in bed watching television.
Bernie:
I wish he wouldn't work so hard.
I wish he wouldn't get angry.
I wish he'd tell me what's wrong.
I wish he wouldn't interfere with my possessions.
I wish he wouldn't move my books around.

102

2 wish I had
3 wish I'd learnt/learned
4 wish I'd known
5 wishes they hadn't moved
6 wish I knew
7 wish they'd never started

103

2 was written by Philip Pullman
3 were built by the Ancient Egyptians
4 was invented by Guglielmo Marconi
5 was painted by Picasso
6 was played by Angelina Jolie
7 was designed by Gustave Eiffel
8 was discovered by Crick and Watson
9 was directed by Akira Kurosawa
10 was discovered by Marie Curie

104

3 The puncture has been mended.
4 The dishes have been washed.
5 Jane Jones has been elected.
6 The rabbit has disappeared.
7 The sculpture has been stolen.
8 The students have passed.

105

2 Nearly £50,000 was taken from the hotel safe.
3 Several of the bedrooms were also broken into.
4 Articles of value were removed.
5 Several pieces of equipment were damaged.
6 The chef was injured.
7 He was left lying unconscious on the floor.
8 The thieves were arrested early this morning.

106

2 won't be overheard
3 wouldn't have been sacked
4 is never answered … are kept … have been written
5 had been watered … had been cut
6 is suspected … has been arrested … is being questioned … will be identified
7 was being reorganised … had been moved

107

2 because it **belonged** to my grandmother
3 *OK*
4 It**'s being repaired** this week.
5 The bridge **collapsed** during the floods
6 someone **will get/be hurt** in a minute
7 but it **didn't refer** to you
8 *OK*
9 the money **had disappeared**
10 Children under the age of seven **are not allowed** in this pool.

108

2 have been introduced
3 have made
4 was shown
5 has been owned
6 was given
7 was killed
8 suffered
9 was restored
10 added
11 doesn't feel
12 was sent
13 hated
14 behaved
15 get sacked
16 will be invited

109

2 was kept waiting for half an hour by my boyfriend
3 must be paid by the students
4 could have been written by your brother
5 is used to do that job nowadays
6 were being employed every week
7 were not informed that there had been a mistake
8 be sent by your company next year
9 was worried by the news about the war
10 hasn't been claimed
11 ever been asked for your opinion
12 shouldn't have been opened by the children
13 must be worn by all visitors
14 must have been changed
15 being used

110

2 's been closed / has been closed
3 's being shot / is being shot
4 's being directed / is being directed *or* 's directed / is directed
5 was seen *or* had been seen
6 was flown
7 's going to be surrounded / is going to be surrounded *or* will be surrounded
8 won't be invited
9 'll be asked / will be asked
10 were employed *or* were being employed
11 'll be allowed / will be allowed

111

2	'll get / will get	7	gets
3	is	8	got
4	got	9	are
5	got	10	got
6	are		

112

2 is thought to be short of money
3 was alleged to have cheated
4 is reported to be resigning
5 is expected to be finished soon
6 is generally considered (to be) too young to get married
7 was thought to have been destroyed
8 are believed to have been hiding

113

2 was planned
3 was unloaded
4 was cooked
5 to be made
6 had been washed or were washed
7 was cleaned
8 was put
9 was being vacuumed
10 have been laid
11 have been arranged
12 have been mixed
13 will be opened
14 will be served

114

2 I'll have it cleaned.
3 I'll have them painted.
4 I'll have it rearranged.
5 I'll have it mended.
6 I'll have them emptied.
7 I'll have them washed.

115

2 I'm going to have my number changed
3 she should be having the plaster taken off tomorrow
4 he's had a fine new house designed
5 I'm having blinds fitted on the windows
6 she had him followed
7 to have it straightened

116

3 When were you here before?
4 Why did you come then?
5 Why have you come this time?
6 Are you doing a tour now?
7 How many cities are you going to / visit? or … will you visit?
8 What do you want to do after that?
9 Do you have a message for your fans?

117

2 how much this guidebook costs or how much this guidebook is
3 where the postcards are
4 what time / when the last bus leaves
5 how to use this timetable or how this timetable works
6 where the museum is
7 when the music festival is or when the music festival takes place
8 how old the castle is

118

2 Is one with a sea view available?
3 have you heard about the special offer we are running at the moment?
4 Why don't you take advantage of it?
5 What have I got to do to qualify for it?
6 How much would that be?
7 Who should I make the cheque payable to?

119

2 And how much do you weigh? or And what do you weigh?
3 And how tall are you?
4 What do you do (for a living)? or What's your job/occupation?
5 So, do you take regular exercise?
6 Do you do any sport?
7 Do you smoke?
8 Have you (ever) tried to give (it) up?

120

2 What **does** this word mean?
3 How much **does it cost** to fly to Australia from here?
4 We can't remember where **we put** our passports.
5 OK
6 Would you like to explain what **the problem is**?
7 How long did it **take you** to get here?
8 Now I understand why **you didn't** tell me about your job!
9 OK
10 Why **don't young people** show more respect to the elderly?

121

I want to move out. My sister **has found** a flat **we can/could** share, and **we looked** round it **last week**. It **has just been decorated** and **we liked** it very much, but **we've been asked / we were asked** to pay a month's rent in advance. Unfortunately, because **I'm working** part-time and **I don't earn** much money, **I haven't saved** enough for the deposit. **I'm going to get** a new job. **I'm being interviewed tomorrow**, so **I have / I've got** to buy some new clothes for the interview.

122

2 'd been / had been
3 'd had / had had
4 'd worked / had worked
5 'd needed / had needed
6 'd wanted / had wanted
7 'd visited / had visited
8 'd been / had been
9 'd spent / had spent
10 'd been / had been
11 'd brought / had brought
12 'd become / had become
13 thought
14 had been
15 was

123

2 wasn't
3 'd come / had come
4 was doing
5 was going to visit or would visit
6 wanted
7 had
8 to come

124

2 was upset
3 wasn't interested
4 had promised or promised

5 hadn't turned up *or* didn't turn up
6 didn't want to see you
7 had had *or* had
8 didn't believe
9 had tried *or* tried
10 had come
11 had tried *or* tried
12 if she believed
13 would talk
14 was going to be

125

Example answers:
was held every night.
(that) we could go horse-riding, room service was available and they served an international menu in the dining-room.
(that) the gardens had a wonderful variety of flowers and we'd love the private beach.
(that) a fitness centre had been added to the hotel's facilities, the tennis courts could be booked free of charge and guests could use the nearby golf course free of charge.

126

2 Where do you come from?
3 I come from Dublin.
4 That's where I was born too.
5 I've been a fan of yours for ages.
6 That's very good to hear.
7 Are you going to the concert tonight?
8 We want to, but we haven't been able to get tickets.
9 Are the tickets sold out?
10 They've sold all but the most expensive ones and we can't afford those.
11 Can they have some at the cheaper price?

127

The email should use reported speech and reported question structures in the same way as the underlined words in Exercise 126.

128

2 (me) where I was going to spend the holiday

3 (me) what I would do when I left school
4 how the doctor knew her name
5 (me) whether/if I had an appointment
6 whether/if his wife had seen his car keys
7 why she hadn't phoned him
8 Rosemary whether/if she would carry his briefcase for him
9 the receptionist when he could see the doctor

129

2 did you say
3 tell
4 to tell
5 would you say
6 to say
7 told
8 told
9 wouldn't say
10 won't say
11 've already told / have already told
12 tell me *or* say
13 tell

130

2 told   6 to tell
3 said   7 said
4 told   8 Tell
5 had said   9 was saying *or* said

131

2 *OK*
3 She **was telling us about** her fascinating trip *or* She **was talking about** her fascinating trip
4 *OK*
5 the receptionist **told us that** the hotel *or* **said that** the hotel …
6 visitors **not to touch** the exhibits
7 *OK*

132

3 entering   6 to be living
4 living   7 working
5 to bring   8 to support

133

2 to ride
3 setting off
4 to lose

5 hitting
6 to try
7 having lost *or* losing
8 to raise
9 to find

134

2 to see *or* to visit
3 postponing *or* putting off *or* delaying
4 painting *or* decorating
5 going *or* changing *or* switching
6 to deliver
7 to send *or* to post
8 to do *or* to post
9 losing *or* offending
10 emailing
11 to help
12 to join
13 replying

135

2 Jason to sit
3 the cashier to hand over the money
4 buying Della the drums / buying the drums (for Della)
5 Charlie finish his homework
6 to reach the shampoo
7 washing *or* to be washed
8 Sandra (to) lay the table

136

2 being shouted
3 to sack
4 to have worked
5 changing
6 to say
7 being
8 to get
9 to pass
10 help
11 to discuss
12 asking
13 to have known

137

Example answers:
2 I learnt to swim at the age of six.
3 I can't help getting angry when I see someone being treated unfairly.
4 I don't mind washing up, but I hate vacuuming the floors.

5 I sometimes pretend to be listening to what the boss is saying when really I'm just daydreaming.

6 I always encourage people to read books which I have enjoyed reading myself.

7 I remember going to the circus when I was a small child.

8 I enjoy swimming even though I'm not very good at it.

9 I expect to have passed my driving test by the end of next year.

10 I've given up going to discos because they're too noisy.

138
2 a   3 f   4 c   5 g   6 e   7 d

139
2 by checking the instructions
3 spending too long on one question
4 trying to see how your friends are getting on
5 by allowing time to check all your answers
6 cheating in the long run

140
Example answers:
2 sitting at home
3 asking their permission
4 offering to help you
5 helping people who don't want it
6 having any proof
7 being late
8 starting a long journey

141
3 go   7 spending
4 waking   8 say
5 arrive   9 being
6 finding

142
3 of looking
4 to risk
5 in persuading
6 to hearing
7 to have
8 to achieve
9 for letting *or* to have let
10 of sending

11 in going
12 about forgetting *or* for forgetting
13 to forget
14 from sending
15 to remember
16 to forget

143
4 had been murdered
5 didn't love
6 didn't murder
7 wanted
8 had *or* was having
9 asked
10 was watching
11 told
12 called
13 noticed
14 had expected *or* had been expecting
15 answered
16 was shouting
17 were obviously having
18 took
19 shouting
20 had gone
21 to go
22 didn't want
23 heard
24 came
25 was still talking
26 heard
27 wasn't shouting
28 phoned
29 talked
30 told
31 had decided
32 was watching
33 take
34 spilt/spilled
35 was pouring
36 didn't want
37 crept
38 decided
39 never like
40 talk *or* am talking
41 had had
42 usually takes
43 took
44 went
45 saw
46 was walking
47 saw

48 was standing
49 didn't see *or* couldn't see
50 was talking
51 didn't answer
52 remembered
53 had told *or* told
54 was playing *or* was going to play
55 walked
56 met
57 reached
58 was looking
59 called
60 was
61 had planned
62 had been visiting
63 let
64 seemed
65 showed
66 shouting
67 were having *or* had been having
68 stopped
69 went
70 had already left
71 got
72 to explain
73 to have
74 didn't listen *or* wouldn't listen
75 was
76 didn't know
77 was talking
78 realised
79 arguing
80 left
81 seeing
82 weren't
83 is
84 have lived *or* have been living
85 used to have *or* had
86 bought
87 earning *or* to earn
88 went
89 went
90 lost
91 was looking
92 met
93 was walking
94 seemed
95 was looking
96 hadn't seen
97 went
98 found

---

99 wasn't
100 didn't even go
101 had found out
102 means
103 left (*must have left* is also possible)
104 was going to leave *or* was leaving
105 to murder
106 didn't walk (*can't have walked* and *couldn't have walked* are also possible)
107 met
108 was still being shouted at
109 has been telling *or* is telling
110 made

144
3 **a** biscuit
4 *OK*
5 **an** omelette
6 *OK*
7 *OK*

145
2 a burger
3 a bowl of soup *or* soup
4 cheese
5 a banana
6 a coffee *or* coffee
7 cream

146
The diary entry should be similar to Jane's. Check carefully your use of a/an before the names of food and drinks.

147
3 the **traffic is** terrible
4 because **of bad behaviour**
5 *OK*
6 Rebecca had her **hair** cut short
7 the **furniture takes** up too much space
8 I give you **some advice** *or* ... **a piece of advice**
9 *OK*
10 was **a less unpleasant experience** than I had expected

148
3 room
4 experience
5 scenery
6 weather
7 day
8 rooms
9 paper
10 experiences
11 views
12 paper *or* papers

149
3 a
4 some
5 the
6 a
7 a
8 the
9 The
10 the
11 a
12 a
13 the
14 the
15 a
16 some
Example answers:
17 In the bathroom there's a shower.
18 There are some pans on the wall of the kitchen.

150
Check carefully your use of a/an/the/some.

151
2 the
3 the
4 a
5 a
6 the
7 a
8 The
9 the
10 a
11 a
12 the

152
4 The
5 the
6 –
7 –
8 the
9 the
10 the
11 –
12 –
13 the
14 –
15 the
16 the
17 –
18 the
19 the
20 the

153
Check carefully your use of the.

154
... and ~~the~~ Malaysia and then go on to the Philippines, where he will make a speech about the environment.
~~The~~ King Juan Carlos of ~~the~~ Spain arrived in London today for a three-day visit to the United Kingdom. He was met by the Queen and drove with her to ~~the~~ Buckingham Palace. Tomorrow he will have ~~the~~ lunch with the Governor of the Bank of England and in the evening he will have talks with ~~the~~ businessmen.
A conference is taking place in ~~the~~ Mexico City on ways of helping the unemployed in the developing world. A report will be sent to the United Nations, but it is feared that ~~the~~ unemployment will remain a problem in ~~the~~ most countries for many years to come.

155
Example answers:
5 All of them were wearing sandals.
6 None of them was wearing socks.
7 Both (of) the men had beards. *or* Both men ...
8 Both of them had short hair.
9 Both of them were wearing belts.
10 Neither of the men was wearing a hat.
11 Neither of them was wearing a jacket.
12 One of the men had a newspaper.

156
Example answers:
5 None of my friends lives in the country.
6 Lots of our neighbours have pets.
7 All politicians are ambitious.
8 Some of my cousins are very silly.
9 Neither of my parents enjoys noisy parties.

157
2 none of
3 any of
4 half (of) ... all of ... any of
5 most ... a few
6 much
7 each
8 None of
9 Few
10 all (of) ... each ... none of

158
3 if anybody **gets** left
4 There **are no** good restaurants, nothing! *or* There **aren't any** good restaurants, nothing!
5 because he **had few** friends
6 *OK*
7 because **all the information** you gave me

8 I could have **any** seat

9 because I **have none** *or*
because I **haven't (got) any**

10 I have **a lot of** homework

11 *OK*

12 embarrassed that **everyone /
everybody knows** my problem

159

2 anything
3 All
4 both
5 none of the
6 them
7 every morning
8 Neither of
9 somebody
10 somewhere
11 little
12 a few
13 no
14 anywhere
15 The whole
16 no

160

2 Antonio Stradivari was an Italian who made wonderful violins.

3 Ibn Battuta was a Moroccan who travelled through Africa and Asia.

4 Marie Tussaud was a Swiss woman who opened a waxworks museum.

5 Joseph Lister was an Englishman who began the use of antiseptics in operating theatres.

6 Sirimavo Bandaranaike was a Sri Lankan who became the first woman prime minister in the world.

7 Joseph Niepce was a Frenchman who produced the first permanent photograph.

161

3 whose
4 who/that
5 –
6 –
7 where
8 –
9 –
10 that
11 –
12 where

162

Example answers:

3 where you have to wear a tie

4 who enjoy rock music

5 which aren't in fashion

6 in which there is plenty of action

7 whose parents argue

8 to whom I can say anything

9 which will fit under the stairs

10 which involved travelling

163

| 3 a | 4 a | 5 b | 6 a |
| 7 b | 8 a | 9 b | 10 a |

164

2 good
3 efficiently
4 hard
5 surprisingly
6 quickly
7 lately
8 fluent
9 near
10 pleasant
11 busy
12 easily
13 different
14 absolutely
15 good
16 accurate

165

3 seemed **unnecessarily complicated**

4 if you tried **hard**

5 *OK*

6 she speaks **perfect French** *or*
she speaks **French perfectly**

7 an **exceptionally** demanding job

8 she's **well** enough

9 *OK*

10 a very **well**-paid job

166

2 the lowest
3 better than
4 worse than *or* not as well as / not so well as
5 higher … than
6 less
7 the same … as
8 more than
9 less than

167

Example answers:

4 Jill collected more than Alex or Wayne.

5 Bronwen collected the same amount as Jill.

6 Wayne collected the least paper.

7 Alex didn't collect as much as Bronwen, but he collected more than Wayne.

8 Jill collected less than Flora, but more than Alex.

168

5 much easier than
6 the best
7 the highest mountain in
8 farther/further north than
9 not as warm as / not so warm as
10 later
11 earlier here than
12 (any) faster
13 as fast as
14 shorter than me
15 (any) better
16 worse
17 as much money as / so much money as

169

2 We went to the cinema and we also had a meal.

3 My sister plays tennis in the park in summer.

4 She's worked for that company since she left school.

5 If you order the CD on the Internet, it will be delivered by post tomorrow.

6 He calls his girlfriend on his mobile every lunchtime.

7 When you opened the box, did you find a note inside it?

8 We were all late for work because of the traffic jam.

9 I'm definitely going to Zurich soon.

10 The meal was lovely. My friends had even asked the restaurant to make a birthday cake for me.

170

3 Craig has occasionally offered to work through lunch.

4 Angela isn't usually in the office at lunchtime.

5 John won't usually do overtime.

6 Craig usually leaves later than everyone else.

7 Angela has hardly ever taken a day off.

8 John hardly ever has sandwiches for lunch.

9 Craig is hardly ever ill.

171

3 Well, the downstairs ones are always locked.
4 We even have a lock on the little one in the hall.
5 most of the windows were probably locked
6 They were all locked on Friday.
7 I knew we would both be out all day
8 I certainly didn't

172

3 was probably bored
4 has never been there
5 often has a rest about this time
6 has almost finished it

173

3 For		8 in
4 until		9 for
5 By/At		10 at
6 During/In		11 during
7 by		

174

Example answers:
1 in May *or* on 8th May
2 in 1983
3 at the weekend
4 in summer
5 after dinner
6 on Saturday morning
7 for five years

175

3 At		11 until
4 –		12 by
5 until		13 at
6 in		14 –
7 at/by		15 at
8 at		16 during
9 for		17 by
10 on		

176

2 at	3 in	4 in	5 on	6 at
7 to	8 on	9 at		

177

2 on	3 in	4 at	5 on	6 at
7 in	8 in	9 on		

178

2 of	6 with	10 on
3 to	7 in	11 as
4 to	8 for	12 with
5 for	9 on	

179

3 in the shade
4 on a diet
5 by credit card
6 by little-known Russian artists
7 at 130 kilometres an hour
8 in capital letters
9 by a wasp
10 like the last one
11 as a motorcycle messenger

180

Example answers:
2 for rich people
3 for new drugs
4 to new people in our street
5 of their teams when they win
6 in modern opera
7 about litter in the streets
8 of going to the dentist
9 of Mickey Mouse
10 on how much sleep I get
11 at my little brother
12 of places I visit
13 in fairies
14 at running

181

2 a	3 f	4 b	5 c	
6 e	7 i	8 g	9 h	

182

Example answers:
2 *e* The bus crashed into the railings.
3 *a* The square was full of market stalls.
4 *f* The minibus belonged to a group of tourists.
5 *c* They borrowed the car from a local family.
6 *d* They blamed the accident on a pedestrian.
7 *h* The owner was upset about having to sell his car.
8 *i* The driver apologised for taking the wrong road.

183

Example answers:
2 's going to throw them away / is going to throw them away
3 's going to wake her up / is going to wake her up
4 's going to blow them out / is going to blow them out
5 's going to work out / is going to work out
6 's going to clean (it) up / is going to clean (it) up
7 're going to do it up / are going to do it up
8 's going to take them off / is going to take them off

184

2 from	5 on	8 with
3 with	6 to	9 to
4 with	7 to	10 with

185

2 get away
3 get back
4 getting in
5 get on *or* are getting on
6 get on
7 get by

186

2 taken away
3 were taken in
4 take down
5 took up
6 takes up
7 took off *or* had taken off

187

2 's going on / is going on
3 go off
4 'll go back / will go back
5 's away / is away *or* 's gone away / has gone away
6 's has gone out / has gone out
7 'm going (to go) out / am going (to go) out

188

2 put on
3 be put back
4 put on
5 put off
6 put down
7 put on

189
2 turned out
3 turned up
4 turned out
5 turn up
6 turn off
7 turn down

190
2 fill it in
3 do not tear it up
4 hand it back
5 leave any information out /
leave out any information
6 cross it out
7 rub it out
8 being held up

191
2 found out *or* has found out
3 has broken down
4 put up with
5 shows off *or* has showed off
6 lets me down *or* has let me
down
7 bring their daughter Mimi
up / bring up their daughter
Mimi
8 won't keep her away
9 have fallen out with
10 run away from

192
2 pay it back
3 close down
4 ripped them off
5 had been held up *or* were
held up
6 do it up
7 brought the subject up /
brought up the subject

193
2 went on
3 went off
4 blew up
5 drive away
6 gave up
7 dropped off
8 riding off

194
2 come back
3 worked out
4 plugged in

5 left out
6 carry on
7 try out
8 turned it down
9 put up with
10 found out
11 were put off
12 cutting down

195
She used to ~~invent~~ **come up with**
all kinds of excuses when she was
younger. Now, she's ~~left~~ **dropped
out of** college ~~without finishing
her course~~. Her father says he
won't ~~tolerate~~ **put up with** her
behaviour any longer, but I bet
Ruth ~~won't be punished for~~ **will
get away with** it, as usual.

196
1 turn
2 put
3 was held
4 crossed
5 brought
6 let
7 making
8 set

197
2 keep up with her
3 run out (of them)
4 made it up
5 get on with it *or* hurry up
6 put it up *or* try it out
7 let us down
8 got on with them *or* gets on
with them

198
Example answers:
2 The children set off for the
playground carrying their
skateboards.
3 The lazy student put off
revising for as long as possible.
4 I tried on several coats, but
none of them was the right size.
5 We took off our pullovers when
the sun came out.
6 The girl switched off her
walkman and put it in her bag.

7 The old ladies carried on
talking all through the film.
8 The tour guide walked off and
left the tourists in the middle of
the market.

199
Example answers:
1 The young businessman set up
his own company making
computer games.
2 My boyfriend turned down the
chance of a job in Hong Kong.
3 The old lady put up with the
noise for as long as possible.
4 My grandfather took up oil
painting when he retired.
5 The workmen knocked down
the wall because it was
dangerous.
6 The gangsters beat up the
gambler who hadn't paid his
debts.
7 The young couple were saving
up to buy a flat.
8 The business closed down when
the new supermarket was
opened.

200
Example answers:
1 We often eat out on Saturday
evenings.
2 The prisoner climbed out of the
broken window.
3 The new student joined in with
the rest of the class.
4 Air travellers must check in at
least one hour before their
flight.
5 The picture has been cut out of
a fashion magazine.
6 The schoolboy let himself in
with his key and made himself
a sandwich.
7 My secretary will sort out the
documents you need for the
meeting.
8 The investigation was carried
out by a senior police officer.